Home Baking for Profit

Over 100 Best-Selling Bakery Recipes

Mimi Shotland Fix

Notice to Readers

At the time of printing every effort was made to assure that all information was correct and offered in good faith. The author assumes no responsibility for any actions you may take in using this information and she is not to be held liable for consequences which may occur. By using the information in this book you agree that no warranties, expressed or printed, have been made regarding the use or outcome of any information contained herein, and agree that the author shall be held harmless for any claims losses or damages which may occur from any usage of the material contained herein.

Other than a brief passage by the press in an article about the book or author, no part of this book may be duplicated, transmitted, stored, or distributed in any way without the express written consent of the author.

Acknowledgments

I had no intentions of writing another food book. My readers and students, however, through thank you notes, emails, website comments and questions, sparked the idea for this one, a companion to *Start and Run a Home-Based Food Business*. I hope that by sharing my knowledge and recipes, I've helped and encouraged new food entrepreneurs.

Thank you to:

- o   Managing Editor Eileen Velthuis at Self-Counsel Press, for seeing the value in my previous book.
- o   Operations Manager Virginia Carrig at Ulster BOCES, where my popular course Baking for Profit originated.
- o   Former colleague Jackie Mobley Caruso, for her help and insight into the technology we so depend upon.
- o   The teachers, administration, and staff at St. Mary of the Snow elementary school; especially principal Miss Christine Molinelli and art teacher Jane Franco; and above all to students Sumar Hart, Claire JinNiu Kenny, and David Diaz, for contributing their charming illustrations.
- o   My wonderful family for their superb editorial work: daughter Gemmae Fix Schiller, husband Dave Fix, and my sister Kathy Shotland Walker. Also Dianne Jacob.
- o   My extended family for testing these baked goods; and particularly my husband, the family lawyer, for his legal advice and photos.
- o   And again, thank you to all my readers and students. I think and care about all of you.

Introduction

Home Baking for Profit

Over 100 Best-Selling Bakery Recipes

Greetings everyone, welcome to *Home Baking for Profit*. The recipes in this book were selected for their popularity and ease of production. You'll find proven recipes from melt-in-your-mouth muffins to decadent brownies, sugary sweets to healthy morning fare. With this cookbook you can prepare delicious and reliable recipes; and make baked goods for wholesale and retail sales at farmers' markets, fairs, restaurants, delis, and bake sales.

If you're simply looking for terrific recipes, you've found them! But this is more than your typical baking cookbook. My intent is to not only give you great recipes with a proven track record, but to also show how to create your own unique products. Part One, In the Kitchen, is essential for learning about ingredients, equipment, and baking techniques. Included are tips for recipe and product development, shortcuts for how to improve your kitchen production, and more.

This book is also for the home baker with the culinary passion to turn baked goods into professional treats while becoming a more efficient baker.

Home Baking for Profit is the cookbook counterpart to my first book, *Start and Run a Home-Based Food Business*. While this cookbook has recipes and information to help you become a skilled baker, my first book deals with the business side of baking. These books are the ones I wish I'd had when I began. With no business background and no commercial kitchen experience I learned the hard way, through trial and infinite error. Now you can start or improve your own food business using my thirty years of personal experience.

I was an unemployed, soon-to-be single parent when my baking career started. Through hard work, happy customers, and more than a few mistakes, my licensed home kitchen earned enough to support us. My business soon evolved into an all-scratch bakery and café. Later I worked in commercial bakeries and corporate Research & Development kitchens. Now, after years of combined retail, commercial, and home baking experience, I've learned what customers want and how to produce them in a faster, simpler, economical way.

Chapter 8   Cookies! Cookies! Cookies!   75

Chapter 9   Fruit Bars and Cookie Bars   99

Chapter 10   Muffins   115

Part One

In the Kitchen

I know it's tempting to go straight to the recipes, but I hope everyone reads Part One. These first few chapters will give you a deeper understanding about equipment, ingredients, commercial baking practices, and techniques. In the Kitchen is also meant to give you a depth of understanding about recipe development that will help you create and mold recipes to your particular needs, whether you use mine as a base or adapt your own favorite family recipes.

Chapter 1

Set Up Your Workspace at Home

You'll be spending a lot of time in the kitchen so make sure your workplace is comfortable, with lots of counter space. Move (or confiscate) anything that's in the way or annoys you. This is the time to tell your spouse, partner, roommates, or kids you're removing their (check all that apply): avocado plants, video techno-junk, the stack of last month's junk mail, or full but unused jars of cooking ingredients bought for those magazine recipes you'll never make.

Each day before you begin, clean off all counters and tables. Vacuum if you own a pet (no one wants to find pet hair in their baked goods) and then wipe down all surfaces. I use a little tub of bleach water (one capful of bleach to a quart of water) as an economical and effective sanitizer. If your tabletops need protection, cover them with vinyl or flannel tablecloths or even sheets. If you require more work space, use fold up tables or a rolling kitchen cart.

Next, establish **safe food** practices. This is your business and your reputation. You're in charge so *you* make the rules for pets, family, and friends. Here are mine:

1. No pets allowed in the kitchen while in production. Move their food and water dishes to another room.
2. Visitors can be almost as bad as pets, since they don't know safe food practices. Explain that there is no touching food, no licking production spoons, and no eating or drinking in the production area.
3. If your family needs the kitchen while you're in production, it's best to have them wait until you're finished working. If they are "starving" have them eat in another room.

Understanding Your Large Appliances

You interact with these domestic devices every day. Think about them as friends. Check on them regularly to see how they're doing and don't overtax them. They will reward you with excellent, cost-effective service.

Refrigerator

Stored ingredients can get hidden or lost inside a fridge, especially small containers or plastic bags; try keeping all business foods in one area. Label, rotate, and keep track of all foods. Keep a small thermometer visible and check it regularly for an early warning alert to problems. Acceptable refrigerator temperatures are between 38° and 40° F. If the temperature begins to creep up and you have expensive ingredients, use ice and coolers until the problem is resolved and use those ingredients as soon as possible.

Refrigerator Freezer

The self-defrost cycle is in a continuous thaw and freeze. That's great for keeping your refrigerator freezer frost-free, but the stored food also goes through that thaw and freeze cycle. Short-term storage, maybe a week or two, is okay but don't use this freezer for long-term storage or you will end up with freezer burn. Your products and ingredients are still safe to use, but off-flavors develop. If you want to keep batters, doughs, baked products, or ingredients (such as butter, nuts, and whole grain flours) for a longer period of time, consider using a chest freezer.

Stand-Alone Freezer

Chest and upright freezers are excellent supplements for baking production because they can save you money and valuable time. However, the self-defrost cycle works the same as in refrigerators. A manual defrost can be annoying, but it will keep your products in primo shape. I use a manual defrost chest freezer set at -10° F. and have a general "floor plan." I place ingredients such as butter and nuts on one side and food (baked and unbaked) on the other. I fill large rectangular freezer-safe plastic containers with baked goods and place them on the bottom of the freezer. I stack them two or three high, with everything clearly labeled with contents and date. I also use freezer-safe plastic zip bags for certain ingredients such as whole grain flour, nuts, and dried fruits. I slide a few of these bags together into a supermarket plastic bag (recycling!) and keep the handles in an upright position so I can easily grab them. If you're a super organizer, keep a dry erase board near the freezer to keep track of contents.

Dishwasher

This appliance is handy for everyday plates, bowls and silverware, but it can take off the nonstick finish on baking pans or erase markings on measuring cups. Your kids, a spouse, a partner, an enthusiastic friend, or your two good arms will be sufficient. Just make sure to rinse off all soap residue since it can cause gastrointestinal problems for customers.

Ovens

You may dream of a commercial range with a large interior that holds commercial-sized pans. Don't worry. You don't necessarily need one for a home-based baking business. The capacity of your residential oven will work for quantity production. Ordinary home-use pans will work fine, too. You just might need more of them than if you were only baking for home use.

Ovens are crucial to your final result. How your products are baked is as important as any other step, from choice of ingredients to measuring amounts to the mixing process. Proper baking times and temperatures will yield consistent results which in turn yields consistent profits.

Electric versus gas baking is a personal choice. The best oven is the one you feel most comfortable using. Getting to know how your oven works in relationship to recipes and their stated bake times is the best way to learn and make adjustments.

Convection ovens can minimally speed baking time using forced air, but work best for dense doughs with a long bake time, such as yeast breads. It's a common misconception that convection saves significant cooking time for all baked goods. (Apparently marketing departments for the appliance industry did a great job here!) The time savings apply to meats or dishes that need a longer bake time. The time saved is about ten percent, and that is obviously most noticeable on items with long cook times. You'll be better off raising the temperature 25° F. in your conventional oven. Higher heat will bake products faster, so test recipes to see which recipes benefit. The higher temperature usually works best on cookies and muffins.

For baked goods with a short bake time, preheating is necessary, since the chemical leaveners depend upon heat to rise and bake properly. Cookies needing a 10-minute bake would still be raw if put into a cold-start oven. Additionally, if an oven is not fully heated, a low initial temperature may dramatically change how the leaveners work. Preheating is a way to standardize recipe instructions since oven preheat times can differ from one oven to the next. For all the above reasons, recommended baking times are based on a preheated oven.

I don't recommend using a cheap oven thermometer because they aren't accurate in reflecting the true oven temperature. Most ovens work by cycling off and on, so your products are baked based on an average temperature set by the manufacturer. Typically, the oven temperature rises and falls during the cook cycle. If you open the oven door (immediately losing about 25° to 50° F.) during the on cycle, the thermometer will read high. But if you open the door during the off cycle, the temperature you read will be low. And the oven will cycle on again due to the lost temperature. As a result, you could get too much top or bottom browning as the oven turns on due to loss of heat.

Placing the thermometer in the front of the oven so you can see it through the glass door will only show you what the temperature is at that particular moment during the cycle. For an approximation of your oven temperature, place a good thermometer in the oven for an hour when you are not baking. Check every five minutes. You will see a fluctuation but it should be no more than 25° F. up or down from your set temperature.

Thermostats in residential ovens change over time and eventually tend to make ovens run hotter. One of the most common complaints with new ovens is that it "runs cold." Most brands of residential ovens have directions in their use and care manuals for adjusting the "offset" of the oven in 5° increments up to 25° F. plus or minus, so you can adjust the temperature setting. But you can do the same thing when you bake, by adjusting your set temperature up or down; leaving the product in longer; or taking it out earlier. So adjusting your thermostat is a personal preference. The only thing that would warrant a new thermostat would be if the oven suddenly didn't get hot enough to cook or it burned the food in the minimum cook time.

When I worked at a major appliance company testing ovens, we used a standard test which is the common recommendation to consumers when they are having oven issues. Bake something that shows browning, like canned biscuits (I remember doing hundreds of these test bakes). Set the oven as the package directs, let it preheat, then bake to mid-package time. If the browning is to your liking, the oven thermostat is good. If you want them darker, increase the temperature and try the test again. If you want them lighter, decrease the temperature and test again. This method works better than using a cheap oven thermometer.

Don't be afraid of two-shelf baking to maximize oven space. More products in the oven at one time will only slightly increase your bake time. Every product bakes differently, so you'll need to experiment. Just remember that ovens need air circulation for proper thermostat regulation. Leave at least one inch between pans and keep them one inch away from the oven walls or your thermostat cannot properly read the temperature. Use double pans if your products are getting too dark on the bottom. If your oven has hot spots you'll need to rotate pans; otherwise, to retain heat, keep the oven door closed as much as possible. Since all ovens are different, use the recipe bake times only as a guide. Always check your items at the earliest suggested bake time.

If I'm using small pans, say I'm baking one dozen small loaves for the market, I always place these small pans on a cookie sheet (or two) before they go into the oven. This makes it easier if I need to rotate, and for retrieving the pans when they are finished baking. This method has minimal effect upon the overall baking for most products.

Here's the basic rule for how to bake when recipe size increases: when doubling the batter or dough for an 8x8-inch pan, the doubled amount fits into a 9x13-inch pan. Once you've quadrupled the 8x8-inch pan size, use two 9x13-inch pans. There is some advantage to using larger, commercial pans, since you have fewer pans to keep track of and there will be fewer pans to wash. However, if you do use larger pan sizes, because of the large quantity of batter or dough in the pan, you will need to drop the oven temperature approximately 25° F. and then bake for a longer time. This longer, slower bake will ensure that the inside batter will set and bake, while the outside of the batter will not burn. Keep testing until done and then keep track of the temperature and time by marking it on your recipe.

For pan placement if you will only bake using two 9x13-inch pans, you have two choices to maintain air circulation and oven efficiency:

- Use two-shelf baking, but stagger the pans so one is not directly above the other.
- Place two pans side by side on one shelf, with the 13-inch sides parallel, and at least an inch between pans and oven wall.

If you have three pans, place two on one shelf, as above, and the third in the middle of the other shelf. For four pans, place two on each shelf as directed above.

If you have two different products ready to go into the oven at the same time, you can bake them at the same time if their temperature needs are the same. Pan placement depends on space, not keeping similar foods together, so it's okay to mix the two different product pans on one shelf. If you have a timer with multiple settings, or two timers, set a time for each product.

Most batters and (non-yeast) doughs can sit at room temperature (up to approximately 75° F.) for short periods, maybe half an hour or so. If your oven is full and you have pans waiting to be baked, most batters and doughs can wait that half an hour. If your kitchen is very warm, however, it may affect your unbaked products, so if you have room, refrigerate products until baking. For cookies, you can divide all the dough into balls, set the balls close together on trays, and refrigerate. When the oven is ready, place the dough on cookie sheets and bake as usual. Baking chilled dough does not significantly change the baking time; you might need to only add another minute or two.

Working with yeasted products is more difficult when adjusting for oven time, especially if your kitchen is warm. Find kitchen areas that are cooler (furthest from the oven and any other heat source such as refrigerator compressor or heating vent) so you'll have some control and can make adjustments. If you don't have enough room in the oven to bake yeasted products when they are proofed and ready to bake, try changing your production method. For instance, instead of forming all loaves or coffeecakes at once, form enough for one oven load and punch the remaining dough down to rise again. Experience will be your best guide, especially for seasonal adjustments.

One last word about ovens: for easy clean-up, many people use foil on the bottom of their ovens. But foil can block the normal air flow which impacts the browning pattern, and the foil can reflect enough heat to melt inside the oven. Use a cookie sheet with a liner (silicone, parchment, or non-reflective sheet) instead, and place it on a lower shelf so it doesn't block air flow. When you do two shelf baking and want to line your oven with something, use one of the silicone mats designed for this purpose.

Getting the Best from Your Small Appliances

Owning numerous small appliances can be helpful for speeding production and saving you time, but they are not a necessity. If you cannot afford to buy equipment, use what you have and make purchases as you earn money from your baking. I was able to start my business without any of the small appliances listed here. I started without even owning a small hand mixer. Eventually, after I had moved into a shop, I bought a 30-quart mixer. (Years later when I sold my bakery and was between shops, I was sad that I no longer had the use of a large powerhouse mixer. I was thinking about purchasing a 5-quart stand mixer when my husband bought me a 20-quart mixer. I was delighted! It sat on a low, stainless steel table, jutting out from the corner of our kitchen, a foot from the wall for easy cleaning. I was ecstatic, but my husband swore loudly every time he stubbed a toe.)

Stand Mixers

Using a stand mixer is nice, but not crucial; it depends upon the recipe. If you can't afford one, start your business with recipes like quick breads and brownies which can be mixed just as fast by hand. For quantity baking, you can hand mix most oil-based batters in large stockpots that hold far more than a stand-mixer bowl. Or purchase an inexpensive small hand mixer which can be used for oil-based sweetbread-type recipes, or for mixing small batches of almost anything. I use a cheap hand mixer when I don't want to lug out my larger stand mixer. Even now, I often use just a rubber spatula for mixing.

If you decide to purchase a mixer, buy one with the highest wattage you can find; the higher the wattage, the stronger the motor. In addition to using it for batters and doughs, use your stand mixer for cutting fat into crust and making biscuit-type doughs. (See directions in introduction to Chapter 12.)

Never turn your mixer on and off quickly, multiple times, to facilitate mixing. This quick start and stop will only facilitate the need for a new starter switch.

Food Processor

If you have a food processor and like to use it, then do; but I don't consider this counter-top appliance a necessity. It can be useful for grating carrots and zucchini, otherwise, for the small amounts of chopped items that l need, it's just as fast if I use a knife and cutting board. For making crusts, scones, and biscuit doughs, I use a mixer.

Microwaves

These appliances are also not a necessity but a great convenience, perfect for melting chocolate or heating small quantities of butter or liquid. If you don't have a working microwave, just use your stovetop. When I make one-bowl brownies calling for melted chocolate and butter, I use a large stockpot, melt the ingredients, then dump in everything else.

Scales

Commercial bakers weigh all ingredients, even salt, baking powder, and liquid ingredients such as water or eggs. This is important for consistency in both baking the product, and in cost. With my home baking ingredients I now only weigh flours for a consistent recipe measure, because flour is notorious for varying in density. This means a cup of flour can be different from pour to pour, vastly changing a recipe and reducing consistency.

I also use a scale for portioning batters and doughs. During recipe development I keep track of batter and dough weights for each size of cake or loaf and write the weight on my recipe sheet; then during bake sessions when I have large amounts of batter, I don't have to rely on sight. I know how many pans I will get from my recipe and I know the cost of each product so I don't overfill a pan and give away extra product.

Once you're in business and making quantity, scales are excellent for weighing flour, portion control, dividing batters, and keeping product sizes uniform for equal baking. Some people are resistant to incorporating a scale into their baking habit because they may be unfamiliar with using them. But scales can provide enormous benefits.

Useful Tools and Supplies

You might feel tempted to visit a restaurant supply store and load up on commercial grade equipment. With only a couple of exceptions, however, you don't need it. Home baking for profit can easily be done using ordinary home kitchen tools and equipment. The only commercial-grade items I use are scoops for portion control, and a scale with 2-ounce increments. I made the rest of my kitchen purchases in local home goods stores. The following list is what I have in my kitchen and use regularly. You certainly don't need everything listed here; a few basic tools and pans will get you started.

Small Hand Tools:

- A bench or dough scraper is excellent for cutting dough and cleaning your workspace. For cleaning, grip the handle from the top and holding the blade at an angle flat against the work surface, push away from you.

- Offset spatulas (design raises your hand away from the product) in several sizes, from 9 to 13 inches.

- Rubber spatulas, spoonula (spoon shaped rubber spatula), and spreaders.

- Rolling pins: I own several but my favorite is a lightweight silicone rolling pin.

- Wooden spoons, whisks, and ladles.

- A small sifter or tea strainer for sifting confectioners' sugar over finished baked goods.

- Dishers or scoops in several sizes, also called ice cream scoops. Refer to the chart at the end of this book for equivalent measure scoop sizes.

Baking Pans:
- Cookie sheets: half-sheet trays (12x18x1-inch), jelly roll pans (10x15x1-inch), quarter sheet pans (9x13x2-inch). I use the half-sheet and jelly roll pans for baking cookies and as trays for holding smaller pans.

- Miscellaneous pans: different-sized muffin pans; round and square cake pans; an odd assortment of pie, loaf, springform, bundt, ring or tube, and tart pans with removable bottoms. For pan substitutions refer to the chart at the end of this book.

- Paper baking pans that make clean-up and packaging much easier. Put your batter or dough directly into these pans, place on baking sheet, then bake, cool, and wrap. No additional pans to wash.

Miscellaneous Supplies:
- Assorted cookie cutters from small to large.

- Cutting boards: three 2x3-foot boards are stacked on my counter next to the oven. During bake sessions I spread them out and have a place for all the hot pans coming from the oven.

- Wire racks for speeding the cooling process.

- Pan liners for baking trays (cookie sheets): parchment paper and silicone sheets. No greasing required – just wipe down and use again.

- Several long ring timers: I use a timer for everything. Everything! And if I leave the kitchen (other household tasks are always calling), the timer comes with me.

- Oven mitts: I prefer the long oven mitts, but there are all kinds of mitts and potholders, so use whatever is most comfortable.

- Several plastic and glass measuring cups: 1-cup, 2-cup, 4-cup, and a couple of gallon measures, plus a couple sets of dry measure cups.

- Several sets measuring spoons.

- Knives: small paring, long serrated, and a long wide blade.

- A ruler and plastic-coated tape measure for cutting cakes and brownies to keep uniform sizing.

- Pastry bags and tips for decorating.

- Plastic lightweight mixing bowls, some with pour spouts.

- Stockpots and a few saucepans with handles (useful as mixing bowls).

- Storage tubs and containers for ingredients and baked items.

- Cloth aprons and towels.

- Disposables: Waxed paper, aluminum foil, clear cling-type film in 12- and 18-inch rolls, plastic bags, paper bags, sticky notes for jotting info and adding to recipe sheets.

Warning: If you need large plastic bags for covering food, use food grade products, only. Do not use garbage bags which are treated with chemicals (pesticides, anti-fungal/anti-microbial compounds, or perfumes). Trash bag manufacturers do not label their "ingredients" because they are not intended to be used with food.

Food Sanitation and Kitchen Safety

If you produce and sell food, you have moral and legal responsibilities to the customer. Whether you are a home-based baker or working in a commercial kitchen, your production habits and environment must reflect that you are producing for the public. Your products should be clean, free of bacteria, and free of foreign matter. The most common useless (and quite unpleasant) addition to homemade products is human or pet hair. Other customer aversions are eggshells, fingernails, small bandages, pieces of paper and cardboard, dirt, or insects (not only in the food but also stuck to icing or in the packaging).

Bacteria are a natural part of our environment and can be found everywhere. In some foods bacteria causes foodborne illness. State and municipal agencies license and inspect food businesses to keep the public safe. They are here to help you, so take advantage of their expertise. Follow your inspector's guidelines concerning proper production methods. Safe cooking and handling of food can prevent bacteria from causing illness. Nothing hurts a business more than a customer becoming sick or injured.

Only sell foods that you can keep at their recommended cold or hot levels until point of sale or serving time. Potentially hazardous foods are those containing meat, fish, poultry, eggs, and milk products. For baked goods this means cheesecake, certain frostings and fillings containing cream cheese, fruit, or butter; cream puffs and custard-filled desserts; dairy-based pies; and meal items such as pizza, stuffed breads, and savory pies. The bacteria that can cause illness live and multiply between 40° F. (refrigerator temperature) and 140° F. (when heat begins to kill bacteria).

Keep your products at their recommended temperature until the point of sale. If you are selling at the market and want a visual display but don't have access to portable refrigerators with glass doors (really, who does?), use an insulated cooler for storage until purchase time. If you want a few items on display, set these products on trays with ice. Keep the ice clean and do not let it touch the food. If you sell products wholesale to stores, make sure your products are kept at their proper temperature.

Kitchen Safety Checklist

Your home kitchen is clean enough for your family and friends, but when producing foods for sale to the public, you must take extra precaution. For keeping a clean kitchen:

- Use good personal hygiene practices and avoid touching your face and hair. Hair coverings minimize unconscious touching.

- Wash hands often, especially after using the bathroom, answering the telephone, or any other activity not related to food production, including after touching your face and hair.

- No sneezing or coughing on food.

- Do not handle food if you are sick (common cold, sore throat, flu, diarrhea, etc.)

- No pets in the kitchen while in production.

- Limit visitors. Guests are not only distractions, but are often not aware of sanitary production methods.

- Wear disposable gloves if you have any wounds or rashes; small bandages are not enough protection and can become lost in your products.

- No eating/drinking in production area which can lead to contamination.

- No direct eating from ingredients, batters, and doughs.

- Keep work area and utensils clean.

- Be aware of cross-contamination. Keep business food labeled and separate from personal.

- Keep a thermometer in the refrigerator and check the temperature regularly.

- Use bleach water (one capful of bleach to a quart of water) as disinfectant.

- Use paper towels which can be thrown away and thus do not harbor bacteria.

- Use cloth towels to wipe up spills. Do not re-use before laundering.

- Control insects and rodents.

- Wash fruits and vegetables before using.

- Be aware that if you live in a warm climate and do not have air conditioning, your kitchen will be subject to more problems with insects, mold, storage, and shelf life issues.

Keeping a Safe and Accident-Free Kitchen

In our hearts, we all want to have a safe and accident-free kitchen. But the reality of a long and rushed workday often leaves us tired, overextended, and distracted. Slow down and pay attention to your surroundings:

- Watch those toes and fingers, use common sense. Wear protective clothing, especially covered shoes.

- Glass containers need special handling because they can break or shatter. Consider using only plastic or rubber containers.

- Knives should not be dropped into the sink where you can't see them. Set them on the counter until washing.

- When taking tools to another location, cover or wrap the sharp edge of knives.

- Keep a fire extinguisher in plain view and easy reach.

- Never stick anything (spatula, fingers, etc.) into a mixer bowl with a moving attachment.

- Make others in the kitchen aware of your rules.

Chapter 2

Baking Basics

In this chapter I'll discuss the factors to take into account when you develop a recipe for sale. You must always think about many issues, not only consumer demand, but also ease of production, availability and cost of ingredients, shelf life, and storage. You must evaluate for taste, flavor, texture, mouth-feel, local and seasonal issues, and overall appeal to customers.

My intent is to give you great recipes with a proven track record *and* show you how to create your own unique recipes. This is an important chapter for learning basics about ingredients and recipe development. My baking philosophy is to simplify the baking process, use shortcuts, and produce products in an efficient, streamlined way. During my commercial baking experiences I learned numerous methods which can help you streamline your own kitchen technique.

About Ingredients

The most important rule in your choice of ingredients is to use only foods that are fresh. I don't mean fresh-picked or fresh-from-the-oven, but rather ingredients that are not old, rancid, or in any way unpalatable. Your first ingredient rule: Fresh or don't use.

The secret to extraordinary baking lies in selecting the right ingredients for the types of products you want to create. The best way to do this is to first understand your choices, and then make a decision. Instead of choosing an ingredient for its brand name, or simply following a recipe blindly, *you* make the ingredient decision because *you're* the baker.

Flours

Most of the recipes in this book use all-purpose flour, bleached or unbleached. My preference is for unbleached, but on a practical level there is very little difference in the final product. I've tested the recipes using both kinds and have found no significant difference between the two.

Use whichever flour you prefer, but please **measure carefully**. Lightly spoon flour into your measure and level off. *Do not shake the cup to level or in any way pack down the flour.* Please be aware of your actions, for most bakers instinctively shake their measuring cup. This action will result in a too-dense, unpalatable product. If you often have trouble with new recipes, consider using a scale for measuring flour.

With the health food trend I included recipes that use only whole wheat pastry flour or a combination of all-purpose and whole wheat. Substitute as your preference dictates. Adjust by adding more all-purpose for the whole wheat, or slightly less whole wheat to substitute for white. (One cup white flour = approximately ¾ cup whole wheat pastry flour. One cup whole wheat pastry flour = approximately 1¼ cups white flour.) Use these proportions only as a guide!

Whole grain flours have dietary fiber, B vitamins, and minerals, so they have more nutrients and fiber than white flour. Whole wheat, however, can taste slightly bitter and the texture can feel gritty in the mouth, which some consumers find unpalatable. The newer whole wheat pastry flours diminish the bitter taste, but the gritty mouth-feel is still there. Additions, such as nuts or dried fruits, help to disguise the texture. If some of your customers are interested in whole wheat, compromise and use part whole wheat and part white flour to reach a wider customer base.

For baking sweet goods with whole wheat flour, make sure it is labeled "whole wheat pastry flour," which is made from soft wheat flour and appropriate for use with baking powder or baking soda. For the freshest flour, I purchase from the bulk bins in busy health food stores, which typically have a higher turnover than pre-packaged supermarket bags. Do not use whole wheat bread flour or stone-ground flour, which are hard wheat and result in dense, unpalatable baked goods. Hard wheat flour works best with yeast.

For other whole grain flours, I sometimes use small amounts of rye, buckwheat, soy, yellow corn meal, brown rice, or oat flour. Many other varieties are available. If you want to experiment with whole grain flours, substitute in quarter- or half-cup increments.

Store all whole grain flours in the fridge or freezer. If you live in an area where people are interested in healthier products, let customers know that you bake with whole grains.

Sweeteners
The most popular choices for sweetening your products are:
- granulated sugar
- brown sugar (which is simply sugar with added molasses)
- varying grades of confectioners' (powdered) sugars
- honey
- maple syrup
- molasses
- corn syrup

Liquid sweeteners are natural humectants and help products retain moisture for a longer shelf life. For this reason I often add a tablespoon or two from the list above to any recipe (usually cookies or brownies) needing this boost.

Blackstrap molasses is more bitter than sweet. It's a dark molasses, so a small amount works as a natural coloring, giving products a golden overtone. When purchasing liquid sweeteners, read the ingredient label. Some brands (even name brand products) sell honey or corn syrup with added water, which changes their function in recipes.

Brown sugar is a baking basic, but in quantity it can be more expensive than granulated sugar. When making a large-batch recipe with brown sugar, substitute by measuring out granulated sugar instead of brown, then adding 1 tablespoon of molasses per cup of sugar. I always do this for large batches, but also keep a bag of brown sugar (in a container with a half-cup measure, for convenience) for times when I'm too lazy or time-stressed to measure out sugar and molasses. It's up to you – a decision on cost-saving versus time saving. For the small-batch recipes in this book, you can just use purchased brown sugar, measure tightly packed; when you're ready to scale up, use the sugar and molasses method. I purchase molasses in a gallon container from my local supermarket. I pour some into a smaller container and work from that smaller container instead of dragging out the gallon every time I need a few tablespoons.

There's also a line of "natural" sweeteners such as raw sugar or Turbinado sugar (called demerara in the UK), a brown unfiltered raw crystal sugar. I like to sprinkle some on top of doughs and batters just before baking. These sugars don't melt so the visible crystals make an attractive topping. Decorative coarse sugars are expensive but they may also be used.

There's a debate about which sweeteners (honey, maple syrup, molasses, agave, etc.) are healthier than others such as granulated sugar or corn syrup; but the answer might be that it's none of the above. They all have no significant nutritional value for the amount of sweetener that we should *not* be eating. (Please think about this statement.) While blackstrap molasses has the benefit of trace minerals, it's fairly bitter and therefore not a true baked goods sweetener. Honey also has trace minerals, but for any sweetener to contribute to one's health we must have more than the tablespoon or two in a bakery treat. If you are concerned about creating healthier products, add fresh or dried fruits, or use 100% fruit juices for the liquid, to boost sweetness levels. It's a personal preference.

My business-oriented opinion: Look at your target market when you make ingredient decisions and produce foods that they will buy.

Fats

Solid fats, such as butter (salted or unsalted, the choice is yours), margarine, and vegetable shortening are all solid fats and interchangeable in the recipes. I use mostly butter, but for some recipes I use half butter paired with non-transfat shortening. The shortening gives cookies a chewy texture and creates a lighter buttercream. If you prefer using margarine instead of butter, especially for vegan recipes, look for a package that states it can be used in baking, since several brands have a high water content. Always be aware that at any point manufacturers may change their formula and increase water content without a label notice. Their formula change may then alter the consistency of your doughs and batters.

You may substitute oil in a solid fat recipe, but because of its liquid state, you will need to adjust the recipe by adding a little more flour. But only a little, since oil makes a thinner batter. I suggest you make the original recipe before making any changes. I use vegetable oil but you may use whichever you prefer. I like using oil because no creaming is necessary so it often makes a quick fix recipe. Many of the quick bread recipes in this book use oil. An added bonus is the (usually) lower cost and long shelf life. When I find oil on sale I look at the use by date, think about how long it would be until I use it, and stock up.

Liquids

Liquid ingredients can often be interchanged, especially if you don't want to use dairy ingredients. Substitute water, juice, coffee, tea, wine, or any of the soy/almond based liquids for milk. Try substituting anything that seems flavor-appropriate.

Many of my sweetbread and muffin recipes use buttermilk. Store-bought buttermilk, buttermilk powder, or homemade buttermilk can be used interchangeably in all the recipes. When I began baking I purchased fresh buttermilk, then switched to buttermilk powder which was cheaper and shelf-stable. Now I make my own by measuring a scant cup of milk and adding 1 tablespoon of white vinegar or lemon juice. I let it sit for a few minutes until it thickens.

For milk – I use two percent but use any that's in your fridge.

For all recipes with sour cream, I use only full fat. Read the labels and look for containers made with real sour cream culture and not gelatin or imitation dairy. You may substitute low or no-fat sour cream or yogurt but it won't be the same since the extra fat makes a more tender product.

Using liquor and liqueurs imparts a subtle, rich flavor without significant alcoholic content. Depending upon your customers, there may be a marketing advantage to using them. If you do add liquor to any recipe, highlight this for your customers. In terms of alcoholic content, using these for baking purposes is similar to using alcohol-based extracts (so they are child-friendly ingredients).

Three of my best-selling liquor-based recipes are included in this book: Chapter 10, almond liqueur in the Berry Almond Muffins; and Chapter 11, raspberry brandy in the Double Raspberry Pound Cake, and a red nut liqueur in the Red Velvet Pound Cake.

Leaveners

Leaveners are used to raise, or lighten, baked goods. Baking soda and baking powder are referred to as chemical leaveners, while yeast is considered a natural leavener. Whipping egg whites is another method to help raise products. Finally, just whipping some batters lightens them by incorporating air.

A few cookie recipes in this book have no leavener, but most use baking soda or baking powder. When using baking soda, crush or pinch (between your fingers or with the back of a spoon) to make sure there are no lumps, which can be unpleasant to bite into or cause your baked goods to not rise properly. Check the date on your baking powder, and if you have any concerns, buy a fresh can.

The difference between baking soda and baking powder is significant. Be aware that one of the most common baking mistakes is grabbing the wrong leavener. Both are white powdery substances. Since recipes typically call for proportionately more baking powder than soda, if you make a mistake and use the soda instead, that recipe is probably ruined.

Chocolate and Coatings

For recipes that call for unsweetened cocoa powder, use a non-alkaline brand (sometimes referred to as "natural cocoa"). Darker Dutch process cocoa should not be substituted in these recipes.

For adding chocolate chips and chunks to batters and doughs, real chocolate is more expensive but makes a significant taste difference. Unless your business is based on low prices, you'll gain more customers with a better quality taste. Additionally, mixing semi-sweet and milk chocolate chips in a cookie dough makes for a special taste. Try it sometime and see what you think.

For melting and dipping purposes, real chocolate has cocoa butter, which needs to be tempered, a process of heating and cooling chocolate so it sets up looking shiny and without turning an unsightly grey.

If you wish, use confectioners (compound) coatings instead. These are made without the cocoa butter, so technically, they cannot be called chocolate, but many consumers are not aware of or don't care about the technicality. These compounds (sometimes called wafers) come in milk, dark, white, yogurt, and other flavors, and only need to be melted before using. Some have a waxy taste and mouth feel, but some brands are excellent substitutes. After several aggravating problems with both humid weather and my tempering technique, I began using a combination of real chocolate with part wafers. All I had to do was melt the wafers, stir, add real chocolate, and stir again. Tempering problem solved.

Flavorings, Extracts, and Spices

When I began as a pastry chef in one restaurant, everyone complained to me about the former pastry chef's awful desserts. I'd not had the opportunity to taste any, but there were photos, and she'd done a gorgeous job. Their complaints were a mystery until several months into this position. The executive chef grumbled that he was ordering too many different flavored extracts and way too much vanilla for me, the current pastry chef. I was using a gallon of real vanilla extract each month, while my predecessor had ordered vanilla only once during her entire two years.

Extracts are essential for most baked goods. For taste considerations, I suggest using only natural ones. The imitation extracts and flavorings leave a chemical aftertaste. Pint containers of pure vanilla are quite inexpensive when compared to purchasing 1- or 2-ounce bottles.

Fresher spices are stronger, so if you're not using fresh spices, either purchase new ones or add a pinch more to compensate for age. The amount and kinds of spices in these recipes may be adjusted to suit your preference. When making small batches, delete or reduce the amount of a spice you don't like; or add additional spices in half-teaspoon increments.

For recipes using dry coffee, use instant powder, preferably decaf, since some people prefer to limit their caffeine intake.

Additions

Additions are all the extras you add to a batter or dough, such as dried fruits, nuts, coconut, or the varieties of flavored chips. Use more or less depending upon personal and customer preference. More additions will of course increase the price but can be offset by charging more for a premium product. If you are baking for family and friends, and cost is no object, more is usually well-received.

Dried Fruits

Most dried fruits can be used interchangeably. Substitute based on cost and your taste preference. If fruits are very dry, soak in warm water or juice for at least 30 minutes, then drain. If fruits are sticky, separate them using a small amount of flour from the recipe. If you like a lot of goodies in your baked goods, double or triple the recipe amount. Remember to adjust prices for the added cost.

Fresh Produce

Fruits and vegetables add color, texture, a little sweetness, and much moisture in addition to the trendy appeal of *seasonal* and *local*. Be careful of their water content, for using too much produce can leave you with a soggy muffin or bread. More flour may be necessary to soak up the extra moisture. For every cup of additional chopped fresh produce, I add ¼ cup flour. In most recipes with produce, you can make seasonal changes to suit local availability. You may also add a little more or less than stated in the recipe. If you're running short, use less; if you have too much, add extra. Use your judgment. I like to experiment with just about everything other than strawberries, grapes, and melons, which have an exceptionally high water and low flavor content in baked products.

Always wash your produce to remove any dirt or bacteria. Even organic fruit may have picked up something between its growing days and your kitchen.

Peeling fruit is a personal choice. If fruit is cut in small pieces, the skin will not be noticeable after baking. Plus, no peeling = time saved.

For health-minded individuals, produce does add a little fiber and sweetness, but not much health. In terms of a "good for you" product, consider reducing the added amount of fat and sugar.

Several of my recipes use applesauce, which keeps the product moister. These products need to be refrigerated within a few days because the added moisture speeds the molding process. In these recipes, applesauce is not a fat substitute. Because fat contributes to a well-balanced, tasty recipe, I still use fat as an ingredient. If you make your own applesauce, use it in the recipes and market them as such. But canned or jarred applesauce, especially the no-sugar variety, works just as well.

Bananas add a moist sweetness to baked goods. Use ripe bananas with a heavily speckled or dark skin, then mash with a fork and use immediately. It's also possible to peel and freeze whole, in the quantity called for in your recipe. When you're ready to bake, simply thaw in the container and use. There's no need to mash bananas that have been frozen – they will fall apart as they thaw.

Nuts

Nuts are a nice addition to many recipes, since they add taste and texture. Used as toppings, they add a lovely visual; but they can also add considerable expense. Since many customers are allergic to nuts and others simply don't like the chew factor, you can often leave them out of a recipe without any problem. If you do use nuts, watch for rancidity which can ruin a recipe, and always watch for pieces of stray shell which a customer could accidentally bite. Store nuts in fridge or freezer to help extend shelf life and always taste before using. A rancid undertone will ruin your product and your reputation. Don't take any chances.

With that said, if you do use nuts, toasting them is an extra step but gives the flavor an added depth. For a visual effect, consider toasting a small amount of sliced almonds to use as a decoration. Before baking, sprinkle on quick breads, muffins, or brownies. These should also be kept in the fridge or freezer.

Recipe Development and Product Development

Recipe development is working on a recipe and making changes until it becomes exactly what you want. Product development, which may include recipe development, is the overall process of working on a product until your changes become a "new" or more clearly defined product. Many times we have recipes and products that are always going through changes and redevelopment.

The recipes in this book were all excellent sellers for my business. They're written in small-sized batches to give you the opportunity to test the taste, texture, and ease of production, without investing too much in ingredients. (Smallest batch size was determined by ingredient amounts for each recipe. For example,

I reduced a recipe based on number of eggs without any recipe using ½ an egg.) If you like the recipe, think about how it fits with your customer base, packaging, and label needs. You can follow them exactly, or use the tips in this section to making change so the recipes are tweaked to become yours.

We all bake differently. There's a joke about when giving ten bakers the same recipe you'll end up with ten different versions. We all bake differently, that's very true; but in your own baking, be consistent and learn your style. If you find something that works for you, then do it.

As for me, business needs have turned me into a no-fuss no-muss baker. I go for the quick 'n easy. I love one pan, quick fix recipes. I hate to separate eggs or whip batters for extended times. I think about production time issues, such as whether I can do part of the recipe and then refrigerate the batter or dough until I'm ready to bake. And I don't like leftover or wasted ingredients. If a recipe calls for one dozen egg whites, do I really want to separate a dozen eggs, and then have a dozen left-over yolks?

My style is a unique mix of home and commercial baking techniques. For instance, I know the home baking rules about using dry measuring cups for dry ingredients: gently scoop flour into cup and level off. But in my style, I don't do that. For years, in commercial kitchen baking, I've only weighed flour. Now that I'm back in my own kitchen making smaller-quantity recipes, I measure dry ingredients using liquid measure cups, but make sure not to shake the cup to level. Occasionally I double check the amount and weigh the flour – which is always the right amount. This comes from practice; your baking habits, too, will eventually result in shortcuts and improved products.

When it comes to trying new recipes, I've learned what can be altered to no ill effect. For instance, in a recipe that calls for two eggs and two egg yolks, I just use three eggs. (Having two egg whites left over is wasteful and runs counter to my efficient baking style.) Or when a recipe uses streusel, buttercream, or a glaze, I always use my own recipes, which I make in quantity and are already in my fridge. And I will not purchase an ingredient unless I can use it before it goes bad *or* it has several uses and a long shelf life. So I won't buy macadamia nuts because of their low use and short shelf life, but I will buy liqueurs, which I don't use often but they do keep for a long time.

Choosing the Right Recipes for Your Business

While this book gives you "no-fail" recipes that worked for me, you may want to create your own, too. Recipe development involves guessing and optimism, and the willingness to pursue a new idea through several attempts. Sometimes it works and sometimes it doesn't. Not every experiment is a success, but you may end up with a winner that brings in more business and a reputation for innovation.

Sometimes an attractive and delicious product doesn't sell because of the size. A delicious bundt cake may simply be too large and expensive, but a smaller size would sell fast. Watch your customers, ask for their feedback, and make adjustments.

For the most part, familiar is what sells. But familiar with a twist is even better. Customers get hooked in by the name and then your version is a winner, far better than a factory made mix or homemade product that uses cheap, imitation ingredients.

Start with a basic recipe that works well for your needs and adjust it. For example, if you want an orange chocolate chip loaf, start with the Basic Sour Cream Sweetbread recipe (Chapter 13). Substitute orange extract for the vanilla, add fresh orange zest, and chocolate chips. Then tweak the amount of flavor to suit your taste. Remember that if you want to experiment (and I greatly encourage this) make the smallest size recipe possible.

Customers first eat with their eyes. Do not underestimate the importance of visual appeal. Use toppings to draw in their attention. Before baking, add a sprinkle of nuts, coconut, granulated or raw sugar, streusel, or even oats. After baking, use a string icing, glaze, or confectioners' sugar.

Quickbread batters include loaves, muffins, and coffeecakes. These batters can be interchanged to take whatever form works for you. Sometimes these also work as bundts or tea cakes. These days we tend to label products based on the form, not the batter classification. So a muffin recipe baked in a bundt pan is simply called a bundt cake. Bake a cake batter in a 9" (4 cup) pie pan and call it a crustless pie. My point is that you can do anything that seems reasonable. When using a pan that differs from the recipe suggestion, fill no more than two-thirds high.

I have several small, 5-inch bundt pans that hold 1 ½ cups of batter, the same as some small loaf pans. But the bundt pans look fancier so customers are willing to pay more. Some large Texas-sized muffin/cupcake pans hold just under 1 cup batter, so two muffins are equal to the bundt or small loaf. Are your customers willing to pay as much for two muffins as they would for one loaf or bundt cake?

Once you're happy with any new recipe you've developed, find people who like the type of product you are working on and ask them to try it. It might be the most fabulous decadent chocolate cake, but if your taster prefers lighter desserts, he or she will not appreciate this recipe. It's also important to find people who will be honest with you. Similarly, if you want to pursue products that typically appeal to a small but dedicated following, such as vegans or those who want only whole grains, find a taste tester with the same preference. At the very least, it's optimal that someone close to you, a family member or friend, shares that preference, since friends and family are more apt to be honest.

As long as we're discussing recipe development and creating new products, think about your own favorite recipes and how they can be used in other ways. For example, look for inspiration from photos of baked goods that look appealing. Then instead of using the accompanying recipe, substitute your own recipe and perhaps tweak the flavor. Or combine your current recipes in unique ways. For example, par-bake your tart or cookie crust dough, spread with jam or your brownie recipe, and sprinkle with streusel before baking. This creative part of recipe development can be fun!

If you're a beginner or intermediate baker, read cookbooks, watch techniques (videos, television shows), take classes, and meet-up with other home bakers. You must practice, practice, and practice. The two main reasons why baked goods seem dry: too much flour was used or the product was over baked. Practice and experience will help you overcome these issues. The most important points are to measure carefully, pay attention to detail, and learn your habits. The best way to learn is to make the same recipes and use the same ingredients over and over. You will learn a lot. You'll get to know when an ingredient is spoiled, what the batters and doughs should look like, how long each product needs to bake, and the optimal time to pull baked goods from the oven. This knowledge will give you immeasurable confidence, which will make you a better baker and business owner.

Scaling Up

Once you have a great recipe and you're ready to increase the batch size, double the recipe and see how it comes out. (Word of caution: never double in your head – write it all down. It's too easy to be distracted and make a mistake.) If you like the way it came out, then double again. If your mixer bowl is not large enough to quadruple a recipe, multiply the original size by three.

For anyone using a 10-quart or larger mixer, you can keep increasing the recipe size until your bowl is at capacity. When I moved into a shop and bought a 30-quart mixer, I typically multiplied my original recipe ingredients by nine or ten. And always make sure to recheck your math. That's where most problems arise.

When you increase a batch size to make multiple items (perhaps you have orders for two large and seven small bundt cakes) you can divide based on visual judgment, or for accuracy either use volume (this entails knowing how many fluid ounces of batter go into each size pan), or weigh the batter in each pan. When I'm working on a new recipe, I get weights for each pan size and write those weights on my recipe sheet. Then I can always make a large batch size and divide it based on that week's orders. For cake pan sizes, see equivalent chart at the end of the book. (But remember, pan-capacity charts are based on how much total liquid volume each pan size holds, not how much batter is used for that size pan.)

Some experts say a recipe can't simply be increased, and they have scientific explanations for why this is so. But in all my years of baking I have never had a problem. Maybe I've just had a thirty-year lucky streak. I've baked thousands of cookies, muffins, breads, and cakes, and all I know is the results I've seen. I'm not a food scientist, I'm just a person who has years of practical experience. The only adjustments I made were rounding an ingredient for convenience (for example, if I needed 3 ¾ tablespoons I rounded up to 4 tablespoons, or ¼ cup.)

Be aware that if you significantly increase a pan size, for example when moving from an 8-inch to a 14-inch cake pan, or from an 8-inch square to a large commercial baking or roasting pan, your temperature and time changes to a lower temperature (25° to 50° F.) for a longer bake. The only general rule is to drop oven temperature and increase oven time when using a larger pan. You'll need to check the bake time at regular intervals until you get a feel for this. Initially, check every ten minutes, starting with the longest time given in the original recipe.

For oven pan placement of larger batch sizes, see Chapter 1, the section about ovens.

Healthier Baking

Most customers who ask for healthy baked goods still want foods to "taste good," which usually means highly sweetened and lots of fat. (That's why we love baked treats so much. That's what keeps us in business!) If you are serious about baking healthier products, (maybe not healthy, but at least *healthier*) reduce the amount of fat and sweetener, use all (or even part) whole grain flour, and bake with fruits, which add moisture and a natural sweetness. Substituting organic or liquid sweeteners for sugar, but keeping the sweetness level high, is only good for marketing purposes. Do the best you can and market your products accordingly.

If your business is strictly health oriented, having a nutrition label with a calorie count is a plus. Otherwise, avoid calorie discussions and concentrate on homemade deliciousness. Highlight your plusses (no added chemicals, handmade, gorgeous decorating) because no matter how few calories a baked item has, it's always too many.

I'm often asked about the use of organic and non-organic ingredients. I prefer to avoid this subject matter since it's a decidedly charged topic. Baking is not affected by either growing process, so it's your personal decision. If you believe in organic or your customers want organic, give them organic. Price accordingly.

Allergy and Health Related Issues

If you're interested in specialty baking for allergies, be very careful about your kitchen and not allowing cross-contamination. Typically, if you want to market a product as, for instance, nut-free, then there must be no nuts used in your kitchen, or at the very least, you must disinfect before working on the nut-free products.

I use all different kinds of products in my kitchen. Some of my recipes happen to be egg-free, dairy-free, or nut-free (you'll see a category list with each recipe), but if customers ask, I let them know that there is always the possibility of cross-contamination.

Many of the recipes in this book are flagged with symbols for certain dietary needs. Other recipes can easily be adapted. For example, any recipe using butter or milk can use margarine or water to be considered vegan (assuming there are no eggs or honey). If you make ingredient substitutions, remember to try it with the smallest possible batch size.

Shelf Life Testing

Most customers think that "fresh" means it was baked that day. But "fresh" really means that a product tastes good with no off flavors or staling issues. A donut is typically fresh only on the day it was made, but biscotti can stay fresh for several months. Every category has its own parameters and every recipe is unique. Part of recipe development is doing shelf life testing.

After you've finished baking your product, sample it so you know what it tastes like on the day it was made. Divide it into several parts, then wrap, label, and date. Set up a schedule and return to the product for regular tasting. Can you tell when there's a difference? When it's drier or more crumbly, then you will know when it's no longer fresh. Muffins, breads, and lower fat items have a shorter shelf life; most customers understand that. For cookies, brownies, and bars, I like to sell a product when it still has at least two days left, so customers can make a purchase and wait a couple days before serving.

Moisture Migration

Sometimes a product will look gorgeous and taste wonderful when it is made, but will not hold up well because of moisture migration, a process where (as the name implies) moisture from one ingredient or area will drift into another. Pies are a good example; after a short time the filling will make the crust soggy. In some cases, however, you might prefer this. A crisp sugar cookie sandwiched with a jam filling will soften the cookie texture for a smooth, softer bite. I like the way this happens, so I never let a customer sample a freshly made cookie sandwich or they will think crisp cookie sandwich is best and the "day-old" soft cookie sandwich is bad.

Quality Control

Never sell anything you wouldn't eat yourself. Sell a bad or contaminated product and you can lose a customer forever, in addition to losing their friends, relatives, neighbors and coworkers. You get the point. If something is burned, no amount of icing or confectioners' sugar will hide it. If something is over- or under-baked, or there is any problem with any product, think twice before selling. And always be on alert for inedible ingredients in food, such as nutshells, pits, hair, and other stray items.

Chapter 3

Production

Included in this chapter are miscellaneous ideas about kitchen technique and faster production methods, with tips I've learned from both home and commercial baking. As a business owner you are striving to increase production, while creating a more professional product.

Production Tips and Shortcuts to Share

I have many years of both baking and retail experience and I understand what customers are looking for in a product. In addition to the pointers covered in each recipe chapter, the following are shortcuts and tips on how to improve products and ease production.

Tips 'n Tricks

- Keep a supply of measuring cups and spoons in your cabinet for all the wet and sticky ingredients, so you don't have to stop and wash them before moving to your next recipe.

- For most often used ingredients (such as leaveners and sugar), leave a measuring cup or spoon in the ingredient container.

- If you're measuring a dry ingredient, simply tap the measure upside down after use or wipe with a cloth. These measures don't need washing after each use.

- To measure sticky ingredients, first pour a small amount of oil into the measure, then pour it out. Or if the recipe has eggs, first break the egg into the measure and then pour egg into bowl. The egg coats the measuring cup the way oil does.

- Make up dry mixes by pre-portioning ingredients and put them in labeled and dated plastic bags or containers. You will save time by having pre-portioned dry ingredients ready to mix and bake.

- Many batters and doughs can be refrigerated or frozen and baked later, using only the amount you need. For example, make a large batch of muffin batter in the afternoon and refrigerate until morning. Then scoop and bake fresh hot muffins for sale at the farmers' market. Or make up a large batch of cookie dough, scoop into balls, refrigerate, and bake as needed for orders.

- Use ice cream scoops as portion control for cookies, muffins, and cupcakes. This ensures that each product is the same size. They will bake in the same amount of time and you will always get the same number of products from each batch. See portion control chart at end of book.

- Use paper baking pans to save on washing. Mix your batter, drop it into the pan, and bake. (Paper bakeware must be set onto baking trays before going into the oven.) The side of each pan has a little tab that the customer pulls off for easy cutting. The paper keeps in moisture so you don't need to ice the sides, and these pans have an upscale appearance. Yes, these are more expensive than baking in your cake pans, but you save time and money when you don't have cakes to de-pan and pans to wash. So this also saves using our water resources. (I don't sell these pans and I don't make a commission on them. I simply remember life before I began using them.)

- If your cake or bread looks ugly (perhaps the icing got smeared or the top appears stippled) these visual imperfections disappear after cutting the product into pieces. I've seen really ugly looking baked goods look perfectly fine after they have been cut.

- Clean up as you go along. If you're like most of us, you hate a huge clean-up at the end of your work session. Try breaking that chore up into tolerable amounts so you don't dread the huge end-of-day clean-up chore.

- To get the biggest batch size and the most from your mixer bowl, increase your batter as much as possible. Then when the bowl is near capacity, gently fold flour in with a rubber spatula and start the mixer on the slowest speed.

- If your bowl does not have a splash guard, carefully drape a kitchen towel over the head, making sure the towel is away from the beaters. This will keep flour and cocoa from drifting upward.

- To avoid greasing and flouring cookie sheets, use parchment paper, silicone sheets, or even foil. I use half-sheet pans for baking cookies, so I buy parchment paper from restaurant or bakery supply stores. These papers can be cut in half to fit the pan. After each use, I wipe them down with a clean paper towel and use them again. I also have Teflon pan liners and soft silicone sheet mats. They all function the same way. Wipe them down and re-use. Unless you get lots of grease or crumbs on your sheet pans, they don't have to be washed after each use.

- Grease everything, even nonstick pans. For convenience I use pan spray. Or mix equal parts flour, vegetable oil, and melted vegetable shortening. Keep at room temperature in a sealed container and brush on as needed.

Use something. Nothing aggravates a baker more than losing time and money for a potential problem we can control.

- Use your discretion; if a batter seems too wet or too dense, adjust accordingly.

- Coating fruits (or any additions) with flour does not help keep fruit suspended in the batter. It's all about the thickness (density) of the batter.

- If your product sticks to the pan when you turn it upside down, try warming the bottom and sides. Either place the pan back in the oven for a few minutes (to liquefy or soften the ingredient that's clinging to the pan) or hold it over a burner for the same effect. (Warning: don't use a propane torch. I know pastry chefs who just grabbed the blow torch. I also know pastry chefs who have set kitchens on fire.) Then gently push a thin plastic spreader as far down the inside as you can and turn the pan upside down again. If this doesn't work, see Chapter 14 – Stale Products, Crumbs, and other Leftovers.

- To keep uniform sizes when cutting products, use a ruler or tape measure as a guide. There are expensive tools for this purpose but they can become misshapen with use.

- Trimming edges – some people cut the edges from their cakes and brownies. This is a personal decision. If you opt for trimming, save the scraps and use them in another product (again, see Chapter 14 – Stale Products, Crumbs, and other Leftovers).

- If you need to consistently level any products because of domed tops, review your recipe and baking temperatures. Try reducing the leavener or temperature for an even bake.

- Testing for doneness takes experience and familiarity with each recipe. I use baking times only as a guide and always check by peeking through the glass door. If your oven does not have this window, check before the earliest recipe time. I use several methods to make a decision: experience with that recipe, overall color, pressing gently on the top to see if it feels firm, and a toothpick (or long, thin, sharp knife) inserted in the center. And then I guess. If I'm not certain, I wait five minutes longer and check again.

- Distractions = mistakes. Pay attention as you're working, daydreaming will get you into trouble.

- Sometimes you just have a bad bake day. Don't let it consume you. Learn from the experience and move on.

A word about "Trough Food"

I giggled the first time I heard this phrase. It put "quantity production" in a different perspective. When you need large quantities of individual pieces it's often possible to bake your batter in larger pans and slice or portion it after baking. This way you don't have to make numerous individual loaves or cakes, fuss with the pans in the oven, and then de-pan separate loaves and wash each pan. So, for example, if you need a large number of individual slices of sweet bread, make enough batter for three 8x4-inch loaves. Instead of using loaf pans bake the batter in a 9x13-inch pan. You will probably only make a minimal adjustment for bake time, not temperature, but keep an eye on the baking the first time for each recipe. If you have a larger pan that will fit into your oven, a lasagna or roast pan perhaps, you can use it, but you'll have to experiment for batter amount. With a larger pan, reduce the oven temperature by 25° to 50° F. and bake for a longer time. Keep checking at ten minute intervals until you learn what each pan size and each recipe needs. Then write it down for future reference, whether on the recipe or an attached sticky note, or make a computer note. This is the kind of information we think we'll remember, but then forget by the following day (or at least after we've baked several other items in this manner).

Trough food works well for the recipes in this book when you need slices of sweet bread, coffeecake, pound cake, brownies, blondies, and bar cookies. After baking and cooling, slice the product. Softer products slice better when chilled, so if you have fridge or freezer space, use it. A ruler or tape measure is also helpful for uniform sizing. Stick toothpicks in the product as guides and make cuts lengthwise and crosswise. Once the products are cut and wrapped, no one will ever know (or care) they were baked in one large pan.

It's fine to use 9x13-inch pans for baking trough food, instead of the larger size. It's what you're most comfortable handling and what equipment you have available. I've been in many commercial kitchens and I've seen everything from large commercial grade pans to stacks of smaller home-sized baking pans. "They were on sale!" exclaimed one owner-manager-head baker I know. "Why not use these?" Why not indeed! And these pans gave him many years of service.

And a word about "Touch it Once"

Some professional bakers are extreme in the view that you should do as little as possible to a product. Touch it once and then move on to other products, they say. Don't spend too much time fussing when there are other chores. I'm no fanatic, but I do use this thinking to help me figure out if I can streamline my process. Does the brownie really need four different colors of string icing or will two colors be enough? How about one pass with a white chocolate, which looks pretty against the dark chocolate top? Just keep in mind your target market, how much time you can afford to spend on any one product, and if the difference is significant enough to help sell the product.

I learned this philosophy the hard way, when I once had a boss who insisted I make peanut butter and jelly muffins to feed the morning buffet crowd: "Fill the muffin cup part way with batter," he began, "drop a little bit of jelly on top of each one, then go back and drop a little bit of peanut butter on top of the jelly, then add the rest of the batter to each muffin, then sprinkle on streusel." That would have been fine if I only needed one dozen for a small family gathering. But I needed to make a minimum of 20 dozen muffins, along with the other breakfast recipes and all my remaining chores. He continued, "And after they cool, add a string icing." It was a cute idea but nope, I wasn't gonna do it. This experience helped me to understand that numerous special touches must be balanced with the extra time it takes to do them. Now, whenever I come up with a "great" idea, I always ask myself if there are other ways to get it done, or if the product can get along without that extra touch. Business is about finding a comfortable balance between what you would *like* to do and what you realistically *can* do.

For the times we need a special dessert for a special occasion, the next chapter will explain when "touch it once" simply won't do.

Chapter 4

It's a Wrap

Sometimes we need a special dessert for a special occasion, or a special gift for customers or friends. Or an awesome platter. The following suggestions will turn your baked goods into special affairs.

Dressing Up Your Baked Goods

Without much additional effort, it's simple to take your product line recipes and make them appear special by changing the size, shape, or adding a topping. For frosting, glaze, or string icing, see Chapter 15.

Cookies:
- Make smaller versions of any cookie recipe.

- Before baking, roll cookies in nuts, coconut, colored sprinkles or sugars.

- Ice after baking and top with sprinkles or decorate individually using a pastry bag and royal icing.

- Sandwich two cookies with jam or buttercream, then dip halfway in white or dark chocolate. Add colorful sprinkles before the chocolate sets.

- Use a string icing. Tint different colors.

Bars, Brownies, and Blondies:
- Sprinkle tops with chopped nuts or streusel before baking. After baking, frost or glaze, or add a string icing.

- After cutting into squares, cut again on the diagonal to make triangles. If you like, cut again into bite-sized pieces.

- Flatten paper muffin cups and place individual pieces in them.

- Bake brownie and blondie recipes in round cake pans. Ice or glaze and sprinkle with chopped nuts. Call it a torte and customers will be amazed at your fancy work.

Creating Trays and Platters

"Trays" and "platters" mean the same thing; these words are used interchangeably. You have creative freedom to craft your own special style when selling your goods on trays or platters. Straightforward rules are simple: foods should be easy to remove and eat, and have a pleasant visual appeal. Remember to use food grade bases and coverings.

Always enclose a blank gift card that has your business info. It's also good to add any instructional info if applicable, such as heating or chilling.

Basic Trays and Platters

For the base, use a plate, metal tray, cardboard cake circle, or basket. The shape doesn't need to be round, but a rim is nice because it keeps the products from sliding off. (Dollar stores have great inexpensive ideas.) Experiment to see what size base works for the number of items. For medium to large trays or plates, make sure they are sturdy enough to support your products. For small lightweight trays, paperware is fine. If you don't want to use disposable ware, arrange for either the return of your personal serving trays or the use of their trays. But in most cases, it might be simpler to purchase disposable ones. You can always add a note reminding them to reuse or recycle the trays after their gathering.

Small items (finger foods) are best, so cut up larger pieces. And if the platter sits for a while before serving, be aware of clashing flavors (think twice before placing anise biscotti next to chocolate brownies, for example). Having at least two layers creates interest. If the foods are sticky or messy, use plastic film, foil, or waxed paper between the layers.

For breakfast platters, use your muffins, sweetbreads, and coffeecakes. For any items you don't make, such as bagels, purchase those along with cream cheese, fruits, juices, or anything you've arranged to supply.

After you're done putting the platter together, look at the overall design. If you find it lacking, add small cookies, small pieces of fruit, dried or fresh (food-safe) flowers, or candies. Consult cookbook and magazine photos for further styling ideas.

When you're happy with your presentation, cover the entire tray with food grade plastic wrap. This will keep the food clean, fresh, and prevent it from rolling off the platter. Use the widest plastic wrap you have and over-wrap entirely, with the film firmly anchored onto the bottom of the tray. If you don't have a wide enough wrap, carefully overlap the center strips so the tray is totally enclosed. You'll need to make several passes if the film is not wide enough. The entire tray can also be enclosed in the stiff poly-wrap, sold at craft supply stores. Position a bow or streamers on top for a finished look.

Make a few practice trays for friends and neighbors. Do travel tests to see how the platters hold up.

Dessert, Cake, and Brownie Trays

Dessert trays and cake trays can be all one kind of dessert, such as a cannoli tray, or they can be an assortment. Brownie trays usually contain only brownies, but you could use a variety of dark brownies and blondies. Most dessert trays are one layer because of their soft, gooey, or delicate nature. A nice touch is to use paper muffin cups in assorted sizes. First flatten each cup, then place the baked item on top, and place on the tray. It's often hard to stack desserts, so if you need to squeeze anything in, push the pieces close together. The paper cups will help to keep each one neat.

Cookie Trays

Cookie trays used to be reserved for Christmas, but now any holiday or special occasion warrants a nice tray. Putting these together is slightly different from other sweet trays because of the typically sturdy nature of the cookie. You can stack them as high as you want. If you've never made cookie trays before, do a few practice trays to become familiar with their make-up.

The easiest way to set up, especially if you're making several large trays, is to have all your cookies in their respective storage containers, lids off, and within easy reach. I place the cookie containers in the center of a large table and leave a clear perimeter for the trays. Then I walk around with a platter and easily grab cookies.

Use an assortment of cookies, but leave out any strong-flavored varieties which can transfer off-flavors to neighboring cookies, such as anise and ginger. Also avoid soft cookies that can dry out. (Or worse, make the other cookies soft. Remember moisture migration, Chapter 2). Sugar cookie dough is perfect for cookie trays because of its versatility. I make at least four different kinds from the same recipe, using colored sprinkles, chocolate jimmies, chocolate chips, or add-ins like raisins and nuts. I also make a chocolate sugar cookie, since chocolate is a favorite and the darker color adds a nice visual against the lighter sugar cookies. I make cut-out sugar cookies in different designs to add interest and fun. Some of these cut-outs are colored, and I often make multi-colored doughs in refrigerator rolls so I can slice a few for added visual effect. See Sweet Shortbread Cut-Outs, Chapter 8.

There are two basic ways to construct a cookie tray. The simplest is to place cookies together by variety, so you have separate "sections" for each kind (for instance, all the sugar cookies are in one section, all the biscotti in another). This works especially well when the cookies have distinctly different shapes. The other method is to build a tray from the bottom up, with the sturdiest ones on the bottom, setting the next layer of cookies between the ones below so they are not stacked one directly on top of the other. You can alternate the different varieties or separate them. For the top layers, a few special cookies with different shapes or colors add interest, or intersperse some wrapped candies or colorful Jordan almonds.

With either construction method, use basic or plain cookies on the bottom where they are not immediately visible, and add the more expensive or time-consuming cookies near the middle and top. The result will be beautiful and you will have kept the cost down for your customer. When you're done, reposition any cookies that look wobbly or clash (I can be very fussy), then wrap as indicated above.

Making cookie trays is my favorite thing to do; it's almost as much fun as eating them. Since I'm the boss in my business, I started a tradition: when the last tray is done, the boss gets to make herself a cookie tray with extras of all her favorites.

Holiday Gift Items

Holidays find us baking certain items that are done only during that holiday, such as Buche de Noel (Yule log cake) or Greek Easter bread. But your usual baked items can be dressed up for any gift-giving occasion.

Gift Baskets

Use any type container to hold contents, including baskets, bags, tins, and boxes. Also consider a container that is a useful or functional part of the gift, such as a colander, baking pan, or mixing bowl. The fuller the container, the better it will look. All foods placed in a gift container should already be wrapped. Standard construction includes placing shredded paper in the bottom of the container and then placing largest items first. For some containers, such as a colander, you might replace shredded paper with a kitchen towel.

If necessary, tape items in place and squeeze in the next items, adding the largest and moving down to the smallest. Continually turn the container so it looks good from all sides. When you're done, place small candies in any bare spots and sprinkle more colorful wrapped candies throughout. To wrap, use wide poly wrap from the craft store, tape, and bows.

Gift Bags

Gift bags can be any size, from a small Number 4 brown paper sandwich bag to a large handled shopping bag. What makes it a gift is the presentation. Use colorful or designed tissue paper, which makes it look more "gifty." The bag doesn't need shredded paper on the bottom. Make sure all items are first wrapped in poly film, cellophane, or food grade containers. A nice presentation is to insert a large piece of tissue paper and extend it outside of the bag, hanging over the top edge. Place your pre-wrapped items in the bag.

Tins and Boxes

Use any attractive tin or box and line each container with food grade tissue, foil, doilies, or cloth. Add the food, making sure to pack tightly to discourage breakage. When finished, tie it with a ribbon or add a decoration (purchased or handmade) to the container, such as a colorful bow, silk flower, or little toy.

Towers

Stacks of tins or boxes are called towers and can range from three up to however many can be arranged without tumbling over. Fill each container, then simply stack your choice of containers, starting with the largest on the bottom. As the tower height increases, the container size decreases. Tape them to each other if necessary. Tie the entire tower with a ribbon and place a bow or decoration on top.

Chapter 5

Bake Sales and Fundraisers

Traditional bake sales involve people donating food, often store-bought, and then selling them in a pre-announced public location. But an alternative is to have a bake sale with a dedicated team of energetic bakers and other committed volunteers who bake and distribute the items. Don't underestimate the rewards of building community by baking together. With good planning, positive community support, and salesmanship, bake sales can be profitable.

Fundraisers are similar to bake sales but can be structured so they include raffles, mail-order, and sit-down community meals.

If you are planning an annual event, take notes on the process and review them after the event, but well before the following year. Have a meeting to discuss changes and improvements, and resolve any issues. Schedule the after-event meeting soon; if you wait until the next year, memories will have faded and key contributors could have moved on before you had the benefit of their experiences.

Baking Together

The kinds of products you choose to make will depend upon several factors – the number (and experience level) of volunteers, available kitchen facilities, holidays near the sales date, and the sales venue. Please note that most bake sales are considered "occasional" and require no health permit, but check with your local authority.

Team Leader(s)

Put someone in charge who has good organizational skills. The leader (or two co-leaders) organize and schedule every step, including contact with the facility, use of equipment, knowledge of local health department rules, choosing recipes, shopping for ingredients, scheduling the production, doing the advanced promotion and marketing (including press releases), arranging for volunteers, and coordinating the sales day. The leader must be able to delegate responsibilities because there's definitely too much for one individual to do.

Volunteers

Find reliable volunteers to take on tasks such as baking, wrapping products, publicity, setting up and manning the sales day tables, and cleaning up after the event day.

Kitchen Location

The single most important ingredient for bake sale success is having a good production space. If you will be producing large quantities, it would be ideal if someone arranges to use their workplace kitchen (restaurant or bakery), a school or church kitchen, or even the kitchen in a local culinary or technical school. It's also feasible (although not as productive) to use a home kitchen over the course of several days. Regardless of which facilities are used, think each step through in detail: reliably predict such details as how long the production time will last, how the products will be stored until sale, and who will transport these products to the site. Every location is different, so the leaders need to go over the details prior to day of production.

Decide on Product(s)

Best sellers are classic recipes created from familiar and fuss-free recipes. Gourmet style items usually move slower at these types of events. Familiarity sells. These are the typical best sellers:

- Cookies: chocolate chip, Snickerdoodle, sugar, peanut butter, oatmeal raisin, biscotti
- Brownies and blondies
- Bars: lemon bars, fruit bars
- Seasonal pies
- Banana and pumpkin breads, whole or sliced
- (Small) chocolate cakes, pound cakes, and bundts, whole or sliced
- Muffins and cupcakes
- Dipped pretzels, fudge, and marshmallow crispy treats
- Non-sweet items such as breads and rolls

For bake sales that are not established events, or when working with inexperienced volunteers, limit the number of products for your first event. Start with one or two kinds of cookies, brownies, quickbreads, or items with a longer shelf life such as packaged mixes (with instructions attached) or candy. Stay away from anything too messy, like apple caramel cake or peanut butter marshmallow squares. If your event is scheduled near a holiday time, use the holiday as a theme to encourage sales. Using local ingredients will also encourage sales and foster community good will.

If you're thinking about turning your successful bake sale into an annual event, consider items such as pies or sweetbreads for Thanksgiving, cookie trays for Christmas, baskets for Easter, seasonal summer fruit pies, or any community-accepted foods such as those from traditional ethnic-related holidays.

Baking Day

Decide how far in advance the products can be made. Ideally, baking is done one day before the event to allow enough time to get products ready. Organization is key to having a productive baking day. Recipes must be printed, ingredients purchased and brought to the baking site, and jobs delegated to appropriate helpers. Individual work stations (measuring, mixing, scooping, panning, baking, cooling, packaging, washing, and clean-up) should have people responsible for those stations. Team baking creates a good basis for further planned events.

Wrapping it Up

All baked goods must be cool before packaging, so you'll need to leave time between baking and wrapping. You can sell individually wrapped items or package your goods in larger sizes, such as putting a half dozen or more cookies in a bag. Remember to wrap for attractive appearance. It may be worthwhile to have a second volunteer crew arrive to help with this chore.

For these kinds of sales you don't usually need labels, since most occasional bake sales are exempt from licensing. But if you're concerned, check with your local authority (either the county health department or your state's department of Agriculture and Markets). If there will be no labels, arrange for table signs with product names and prices as a customer courtesy.

Sales Location and Event Date

When you choose a day and time for the bake sale, check the calendar for any special happenings to watch out for competing events. Two good locations are either weekends in front of malls or busy stores; or lunchtimes in downtown business districts. High traffic areas are nice if you are prepared with enough products and volunteers for the posted hours. You will need permission to set up in any space whether public or private.

Another option is to enlist a network of like-minded organizations or agencies that support your cause. For instance, if the bake sale will raise money for community food banks, perhaps your area churches, temples, and synagogues would help by letting you sell products after their religious services.

Advertise

If your event is a charity fundraiser, ask the local media (newspaper, radio, hometown websites) to mention the sale. Ask folks to post it on their local blogs and send out email notices to any community bulletin boards.

Sales Day

Make a list of all the items you'll need: folding tables, tablecloths, cake stands, prepared signs, markers and paper for more signs, change for customers and a cash box (or system of who keeps the money), and bags for customers to take home items. If there's seating, have little plates and forks with napkins. Think about whether to serve drinks along with the baked goods, such as coffee, tea, soda, or lemonade.

Provide a checklist for safe food handling procedures. If you will be serving slices of anything, it's preferable to have them pre-sliced. Otherwise, use plastic knives. Be prepared with hand sanitizer, extra paper towels and a container of bleach water for rinsing utensils and wiping surfaces. One capful of bleach per quart of water should be enough.

Have enough volunteers to handle sales, at least two people per shift. Having kids help out is always a big plus. People love to see kids helping at bake sales.

Set prices for easy exchange of money. Consider rounding all sales to the nearest quarter or half-dollar. Decide on a policy for accepting customer checks.

Set up your table by dividing products by type, so it's easy for customers to scan and settle on purchases. Be creative about the display. Vary the heights of products and create tiers using cake stands, bowls turned upside down, or simply place boxes on the table under the tablecloth. Leave room around the table perimeter so customers can set down their purchases. Remember, people eat with their eyes first. Make sure the table looks nice and the food is professionally presented.

Customer service counts. Be nice to everyone, even cranky customers.

People can be quite generous at charity events, but when you want to sell them something they don't want, psychologically they feel it's polite and acceptable to say, "No thank you, I don't eat those foods." But they are willing to help a good cause if you provide an opportunity for them to make a simple donation. I passed by a bake sale recently (okay, I saw the advertisement and headed over on purpose). They had a brilliant idea: a large cookie jar with a sign prominently displayed that said, "COUNTING CALORIES? Make a donation and skip the Sugary Treats." How inspired! The jar was filled with $5 and $10 bills.

Food Fundraisers

Bake sales are the most popular way to raise money with food, but there are other ways. Some are variations of the classic one-day bake sale, such as the yearly Share our Strength sale, while others involve preparation of meals, such as pancake breakfasts, clambakes, and food booths at events such as carnivals. And most of us are familiar with organizations that fundraise by reselling purchased factory made products such as cookie dough, cheesecakes or candies.

But why use factory made, mass-produced foods as fundraisers when you can raise community money *and* promote the idea of local? In addition to offering made-from-scratch foods, you're in the position of fostering community pride by keeping all the money within your community. With a little ingenuity and committed volunteers, there are other ways to sponsor local food fundraisers.

In school settings with fundraisers for clubs, PTA's, or special education-related projects, the customer base is ready-made. Instead of selling factory-made unhealthy candies and junk foods, put together a group of motivated parents, use the school kitchen facilities, and bake sellable products together.

For social service organizations that need on-going sales and a much-needed source of income, start a regularly scheduled club that bakes together. You can make a single category (cookies, muffins, or cakes) or a rotating group of baked goods. The bake sale can be done monthly, quarterly, or any way that seems manageable. You can also have a list of customers who pre-purchase products to be delivered on a holiday or special occasion such as a birthday or anniversary. With a club, selling by subscription means you always know how much to prepare instead of guessing, then hoping that everything sells.

To reach a wider audience, advertise through community organizations, by newsletter, blog, or Facebook page, posters, and word-of-mouth. Supporting local causes is popular. For shortcuts and tips about baking and selling scratch-made products through fundraisers, please read Chapters 2, 3, and 4.

Part Two

Recipes

In the next few chapters you'll find more than 100 of my best-selling recipes. Some we baked and sold daily, while some featured local produce and were strictly seasonal. Others were rotated weekly because we didn't have enough display room to sell every product every day.

Many of these recipes are my own, since I enjoy the opportunity to create new products. Some recipes came from family and friends and a few were inspired by cookbooks. When I remembered the recipe origin I noted it with the recipe. My apologies if I have neglected to cite a cookbook or thank anyone, especially friends who have passed through my life.

Several recipes are from Saraly, my best baker, ever. She was a grandmother, retired county employee, and a passionate home baker. I met her when I moved my home baking business into a small neighbor shop and posted a sign at the local food co-op: *Help wanted in exchange for baked goods*. Over the years Saraly shared many of her recipes and baking tips, doing so with sincere pleasure and warm generosity.

All of these products began as small quantity home recipes. I scaled them up and tweaked them for large bakery production, using a 30- or 60- quart mixer. I've since lost track of the original small-scale copies, but I did keep my bakery production cards, now old and stained but legible. For the recipes in this book I scaled down from the large batch size (ex. start with five pounds of butter, add a flat of eggs) to home baking size. This way you can test using a small batch size to see if the baked good fits your palate and your needs, without costing too much.

So who needs another chocolate chip cookie or brownie recipe? In deciding which recipes to include, I almost didn't add some of my bestsellers, which are bakery classics. These recipes are standard baked goods and I assumed home bakers already had their own favorites. But my students insisted that they were especially interested in what worked for me. Standard fare equals great sellers and since recipes vary, they wanted mine. I assume you do, too.

Within each chapter I selected similar recipes but made from different ingredients. You'll find some coffeecake recipes made with oil and some with butter. The brownie recipes use unsweetened chocolate, cocoa, or semi-sweet chocolate. This way, if you have ingredient preferences, I've given you a choice.

In the last chapter, you'll find a few basic recipes for streusels, buttercream frosting, glazes, and string icing (a thin form of glaze applied in a string-like appearance). These recipes are used many times in this book for a variety of products. For ease of production, make these in large batches and keep refrigerated so they are always ready to use.

How to Use this Book

For an in-depth discussion of ingredients, please read *About Ingredients* in Chapter 2. Here are some of the most important things to know for recipes in this book:

- Unless otherwise noted, recipes use softened butter.
- Use large eggs.
- Use any vegetable oil you prefer.
- When the recipe simply states flour, it's referring to all-purpose.
- All baked goods need to cool before wrapping and storing.
- It goes without saying (right?) that if you make a substitution, the results will differ.

Shelf life will vary based on your ingredients, style of baking, and storage method. *Several days* means more than two, but less than a week.

Yield refers to pan size. Usually, an 8x8-inch pan has 9 pieces, while a 9x13-inch pan has 12 pieces. You will determine the serving size based on your customers and the price you will charge. These pieces may be cut into squares, rectangles, or (dare to be different) triangles.

Insider Tips denotes ways to vary the recipe in terms of pan size, deletions, or additions.

Quick fix (no relation to the Fix family) denotes a recipe that is especially fast to assemble and can be mixed by hand. If you read my blog, http://baking-fix.com/thefix, you're probably familiar with this notation.

CATEGORIES for special diets comprise:

- Whole grain (made with oats, cornmeal, or at least half whole wheat flour)
- Dairy free
- Egg free

- Nut free
- Gluten free
- Vegan

The last two categories were not popular while my retail business was open, but I do have a few noted recipes. If those categories are of interest to you, feel free to make ingredient substitutions based on dietary needs.

My recipes assume you have previous baking experience. If any of the recipes don't have enough detail for your skill level (for example, perhaps you're still not sure how to measure flour or melt chocolate) please refer to a basic baking cookbook.

Many photos for these recipes are posted on my blog, http://bakingfix.com/ thefix where you will find a separate page for this book.

Chapter 6

Brownies and Blondies

Brownies and blondies are not only popular, but some of the easiest and fastest baked goods to make. They're adaptable to innumerable variations and easy to dress up. When you're short on time but must churn out products, these can help any time-stressed schedule. These suggestions apply to all the recipes in this chapter.

Tips for baking:
- To lift brownies from pan for easy cutting, line pan with foil or parchment paper and extend over the pan edges. When cool, run a knife around the inside edges and lift out using the foil or paper handles.

- Bake with a parchment liner cut to fit the pan. When cool, run a knife around inside edge and flip pan upside down onto a cutting board, peel off the paper, place another board on the bottom, and flip over.

- Bake in paper or aluminum trays and package with a plastic knife.

- Bake in muffin cups.

Tips for handling:
- Very moist brownies might smear when cut. If so, refrigerate and cut while cold. Or dip knife in warm or hot water, wipe down blade, make cut, and repeat.

- Cutting off the crust is a personal decision. Some customers like the edges, some don't. If you prefer to cut all edges, cut as close as possible to the edge. Save and use the scraps (see Chapter 14 on Stale Products, Crumbs, and other Leftovers).

- Wrap brownies and blondies well to keep them from drying out. If stacking, place waxed paper, parchment, or plastic film between layers.

Variations:
- For visual appeal, sprinkle tops with chopped nuts, coconut, or chocolate bits.

- During the winter holidays, add candy-coated chocolates, glace cherries, or mixed candied fruits to any batter.

- For a dense, sweet "torte," bake in a round cake pan.

- Frost with buttercream or a string icing.

- Cut in triangles by first cutting into squares, then cutting diagonally.

- For making trays, use paper muffin cups to hold each piece. Flatten the cup, then place the brownie on top.

Most brownies and blondies can be cut diagonally.

Almond Flour Brownies

This brownie batter makes a true flourless torte. Bake in a cake pan for special occasion orders.

Yield: 1 8x8-inch pan

- ¼ pound (1 stick) butter, melted
- 1 cup sugar
- 2 large eggs
- 1 teaspoon vanilla
- 1 cup almond meal flour
- 6 tablespoons cocoa
- ¼ teaspoon baking soda
- ¼ teaspoon salt

1. Preheat oven to 350° F. and grease pan.

2. Combine butter, sugar, eggs, and vanilla in a medium bowl.

3. Stir together almond meal, cocoa, baking soda, and salt in a small bowl. When thoroughly mixed, blend into butter mixture.

4. Spread batter evenly in prepared baking pan. Bake 25 to 35 minutes until top feels firm when gently pressed and a toothpick inserted near center comes out clean. Keeps five days at room temperature.

INSIDER TIPS
- Quick fix
- Top each brownie piece with a whole or sliced almond.
- Bake in cake pan and ice with buttercream (Chapter 15).
- Instead of almond meal substitute peanut flour.

CATEGORIES
- Gluten free

Brownie Peanut Butter Cups

This recipe was inspired by the classic peanut butter cup candy. It's a moist brownie baked as a muffin with a sturdy peanut butter filling.

Yield: 12 medium brownie cups

Filling

- 2 tablespoons butter
- $^2/_3$ cup peanut butter, creamy or crunchy
- 1 cup miniature marshmallows

Brownie

- $^2/_3$ cup (4 ounces) semi-sweet chocolate
- ¼ pound (1 stick) butter
- 1 cup brown sugar
- 3 large eggs
- 1 teaspoon vanilla
- $^1/_8$ teaspoon salt
- ¼ teaspoon baking soda
- ¼ cup cocoa
- ¾ cup flour

1. Preheat oven to 350° F. and line 12 muffin cups with paper.

2. To make the filling, melt butter in a small saucepan over medium heat. Stir in peanut butter and add marshmallows. Stir over low heat until thick and blended. Remove from heat.

3. For the brownie batter, melt together the chocolate and butter in another saucepan over low heat. Cool slightly, then beat in the sugar, eggs, vanilla, salt, and baking soda.

4. Mix the cocoa and flour in a small bowl. Add to the chocolate batter and blend well.

5. Reserve about ¾ cup of batter (enough for a tablespoon per brownie) and divide the rest evenly amongst the 12 cups. Spoon equal amounts of peanut butter filling into the center of each cup and press down. Top each cup with some of the remaining batter.

6. Bake for 25 to 30 minutes. Brownies are done when the tops appear set. If you like extra moist brownies, bake a few minutes less. Keeps for several days.

INSIDER TIPS

- Top each brownie with a spoonful of buttercream, then press in half of a peanut butter cup candy, cut side down.

Chocolate Raspberry Brownies

Customers love the combination of raspberry and chocolate. These brownies are especially attractive when topped with a raspberry buttercream.

Yield: 1 8x8-inch pan

Filling

- $1/3$ cup raspberry jam, preferably seedless
- 4 ounces cream cheese, softened

Brownie

- 3 squares (3 ounces) unsweetened chocolate
- ¼ pound (1 stick) butter
- 1 ½ cups brown sugar
- 2 large eggs
- 1 ½ teaspoons vanilla
- ¾ cup flour
- ½ teaspoon baking powder
- ½ teaspoon salt
- 1-2 cups raspberry buttercream, optional (Chapter 15)

1. Mix jam and cream cheese together in a small bowl and set aside.
2. Preheat oven to 350° F. and grease pan.
3. Melt chocolate and butter in large saucepan on low heat, and then cool for five minutes. Beat in sugar, eggs, and vanilla. Mix in flour, baking powder, and salt.
4. Spread batter evenly in the prepared baking pan. Drop large spoonfuls of filling on top of batter. Swirl slightly to mix.
5. Bake 40 to 50 minutes, or until the bars feel firm when pressed lightly with your finger and the brownie pulls away from the sides of the pan. The cream cheese/raspberry mixture darkens while baking and develops cracks at the end of the bake time.
6. Cool thoroughly. If using, top with raspberry buttercream. Refrigerate before cutting. Brownies stay moist for several days.

INSIDER TIPS

- Quick fix

CATEGORIES

- Nut free

Coconut Chocolate Chunk Blondies

Sometimes customers get tired of "the same old thing" so I created a variation of the chocolate chip blondie. The large chocolate chunks are a nice contrast to the soft coconut, but you can substitute chips if you prefer.

Yield: 1 8x8-inch pan

- ¼ pound (1 stick) butter, melted
- 1 cup sugar
- 1 tablespoon corn syrup
- 1 large egg
- 1 teaspoon vanilla
- 1 ¼ cups flour
- 1 teaspoon baking powder
- $^{1}/_{8}$ teaspoon salt
- 1 cup semi-sweet chocolate chunks
- 1 ½ cups sweetened flaked coconut

1. Preheat oven to 350° F. and grease pan.

2. Combine butter, sugar, corn syrup, egg, and vanilla in a medium bowl. Stir in flour, baking powder, and salt. When thoroughly mixed, stir in chocolate chunks and most of the coconut, reserving some for sprinkling on top.

3. Press dough evenly into the prepared pan. Sprinkle on the reserved coconut.

4. Bake 20 to 30 minutes until the top is a light golden brown and feels firm when gently pressed. Keeps five days at room temperature.

INSIDER TIPS
- Quick fix

CATEGORIES
- Nut free

Cookies 'n Cream Cheesecake Brownies

One day at my shop the baking schedule included brownies, cheesecake, and chocolate crème-filled sandwich cookies. I decided to try including them in one pan. That's how recipes ideas begin.

Yield: 1 8x8-inch pan

Filling

- 8 ounces cream cheese, softened
- ¼ cup sugar
- 6-8 chocolate sandwich cookies, chopped

Brownies

- ¼ pound (1 stick) butter, melted
- 1 cup sugar
- 2 large eggs
- 1 teaspoon vanilla
- ½ cup flour
- 6 tablespoons cocoa
- ½ teaspoon baking powder
- ¼ teaspoon salt

1. Preheat oven to 350° F. and grease pan.
2. For the filling, beat cream cheese and sugar in a large bowl, then stir in most of the chopped cookies, reserving some to sprinkle on top.
3. For the brownies, combine butter, sugar, eggs, and vanilla in a medium bowl. In a separate bowl, stir together flour, cocoa, baking powder, and salt. Add to butter mixture and beat until well blended.
4. Spread batter in prepared pan. Drop filling in several places on the brownie batter. Swirl batters in brief strokes to barely combine. Sprinkle on reserved cookies.
5. Bake 30 to 40 minutes, until brownies feel firm on top and begin pulling away from the pan sides.
6. Chill before cutting. Store refrigerated up to five days.

INSIDER TIPS

- Sprinkle finely chopped chocolate over top after baking.

CATEGORIES

- Nut free

Espresso Brownies

When I was growing up my mom made brownies like these using an old Crisco recipe booklet, circa 1948. I only made a few changes (butter instead of shortening, more chocolate) and added coffee flavor.

Yield: 1 8x8-inch pan

- 6 ounces (1 ½ sticks) butter
- 1 ½ cups sugar
- 3 large eggs
- 3 squares (3 ounces) unsweetened chocolate, melted and cooled
- 1 teaspoon vanilla
- 1 cup flour
- 1 tablespoon espresso powder (or instant coffee granules)
- ½ teaspoon baking powder
- ½ teaspoon salt

1. Preheat oven to 350° F. and grease pan.

2. Cream butter, sugar, and eggs in a medium bowl. Stir in melted chocolate and vanilla. Add flour, coffee powder, baking powder, and salt, stirring until thoroughly combined.

3. Pour into prepared pan, spread into corners, and bake 30 to 35 minutes, until the top feels firm when lightly pressed. Keeps five days.

INSIDER TIPS
- Quick fix
- Excellent with a mocha buttercream (Chapter 15).
- For double chocolate brownies, add 1 cup chocolate chunks.

CATEGORIES
- Nut free

Fruitcake Blondies

I know all the fruitcake jokes but there's definitely a market for this traditional holiday treat. The rum extract is an important part of this recipe. Just a little gives a necessary hint of flavor.

Yield: 1 9x13-inch pan

- ½ pound (2 sticks) butter
- 1 $^2/_3$ cups granulated sugar
- 2 tablespoons corn syrup
- 2 large eggs
- 1 teaspoon vanilla extract
- $^1/_8$ teaspoon rum extract
- 2 ¼ cups flour
- 1 teaspoon baking powder
- ½ teaspoon salt
- 2 cups chopped candied fruits
- ½ cup nuts

1. Preheat oven to 350° F. and grease baking pan.

2. Cream butter and sugar in a medium bowl. Add corn syrup, eggs, vanilla, and rum extracts, creaming well until combined.

3. Add flour, baking powder, and salt. Mix until all dry ingredients are incorporated. Stir in fruits and nuts.

4. Scrape into prepared pan, spread into corners, and smooth the top. Bake 25 to 35 minutes, until a medium golden brown and the blondie feels firm when lightly pressed. If the bottom seems too dark but it's not finished baking, set the brownie pan on another baking sheet. Keeps several days.

INSIDER TIPS
- Quick fix

Knock-Your-Socks-Off Chocolate Brownies

This recipe is versatile and super easy to mix, with way too much chocolate.

Yield: 1 8x8-inch pan

- ½ cup oil
- 1 cup brown sugar
- 2 large eggs
- 1 teaspoon vanilla
- ¾ cup flour
- ¼ cup cocoa
- ½ teaspoon baking powder
- ¼ teaspoon salt
- 1 cup (6-ounce bag) semi-sweet chocolate chips
- 1 cup (6-ounce bag) milk chocolate chips

1. Preheat oven to 350° F. and grease pan.

2. Beat together oil, sugar, eggs, and vanilla in a medium bowl.

3. Combine flour, cocoa, baking powder, and salt in another bowl. Mix until there are no lumps of cocoa. Add to the oil mixture and beat until thoroughly combined. Stir in the two kinds of chips.

4. Pour into prepared pan and bake 35 to 40 minutes, until the top feels firm when gently pressed. Keeps up to five days.

INSIDER TIPS
- Quick fix
- Add 2 teaspoons instant coffee powder.

CATEGORIES
- Nut free

Marshmallow Hot Chocolate Brownies

A few of us worked late one summer night finishing up orders. We bought a half-gallon of ice-cream and some toppings and a new brownie flavor was created. It's messy but a customer favorite.

Yield: 1 8x8-inch pan

- ½ pound (2 sticks) butter, melted
- 1 ¾ cups brown sugar
- 3 large eggs
- 1 ½ teaspoons vanilla
- 1 cup flour
- ½ cup plus 2 tablespoons cocoa
- ¼ teaspoon salt
- ¼ teaspoon baking soda
- 1 cup mini marshmallows
- 1 cup (6-ounce bag) chocolate chips
- ½ cup store bought caramel or chocolate ice cream topping, warmed

1. Preheat oven to 350° F. and grease pan.

2. Combine melted butter, sugar, eggs, and vanilla in a medium bowl.

3. Combine flour, cocoa, salt, and baking soda in another bowl. Mix until there are no lumps of cocoa. Add to the butter mixture and beat until combined.

4. Pour into the prepared pan and bake 30 to 40 minutes or until the top feels firm when lightly pressed and the brownie pulls away from the sides of the pan.

5. When cool, use some of the topping to thinly glaze the brownie. Add mini-marshmallows and chips and press down. Dip the tines of a fork into the remaining topping and drizzle over the brownie.

6. If these are too moist for easy cutting, refrigerate until firm. Keeps several days.

INSIDER TIPS
- Add chopped glace cherries during the winter holidays.
- Bake and sell in individual pans with a plastic fork.
- Excellent if heated and served warm.

CATEGORIES
- Nut free

Peanut Butter Blondies

A basic peanut butter blondie that works well with additions.

Yield: 1 8x8-inch pan

- ¼ pound (1 stick) butter
- ½ cup peanut butter, crunchy or creamy
- 1 cup brown sugar
- 2 large eggs
- 2 teaspoons vanilla
- 1 cup flour
- 1 teaspoon baking powder
- ¼ teaspoon salt
- 1 cup chopped peanuts, optional

1. Preheat oven to 350° F. and grease pan.

2. Cream softened butter, peanut butter, and sugar in a medium bowl. Add eggs and extract and cream well. Mix in flour, baking powder, and salt. Scrape bowl to incorporate all ingredients.

3. Add peanuts, if using, and mix until evenly combined. The dough will be very stiff.

4. Spread evenly in pan and bake 35 to 40 minutes, until the top is a golden brown and feels firm when gently pressed. Keeps several days at room temperature.

INSIDER TIPS
- Quick fix
- Add 1 cup peanut butter chips or chocolate chips.
- For whole grain, substitute ¾ cup whole wheat pastry flour for the all-purpose flour.

Snickerdoodle Blondies

I created this recipe when a customer requested cinnamon blondies for her wedding reception. I made a few extra pans for my bakery customers. The blondies sold so well they became part of my rotating menu.

Yield: 1 8x8-inch pan

- 6 ounces (1 ½ sticks) butter
- 1 ½ cups brown sugar
- 2 large eggs
- 1 ½ teaspoons vanilla
- 2 cups flour
- 1 ½ teaspoons baking powder
- 1 teaspoon cinnamon
- ½ teaspoon salt
- 2 tablespoons cinnamon sugar

1. Preheat oven to 350° F. and grease baking pan.

2. Cream butter and sugar in a medium bowl. Add eggs and vanilla, creaming well until combined. Add flour, baking powder, cinnamon, and salt. Mix until all dry ingredients are incorporated.

3. Spread half of the batter into the prepared pan. Sprinkle with one tablespoon cinnamon sugar and refrigerate for a few minutes to harden the dough. Scrape the remaining dough into the pan and gently spread the dough over the sugar. Smooth the top, then sprinkle on the other tablespoon of cinnamon sugar.

4. Bake 35 to 45 minutes, until a medium golden brown and the blondie feels firm when lightly pressed. Keeps several days.

INSIDER TIPS
- Quick fix

CATEGORIES
- Nut free

Spiced Apple Blondies

For people who don't like dense brownies and blondies (I know, hard to believe), attract new customers with a fruit blondie. It's tender, spicy, and cake-like. Excellent topped with a spiced buttercream.

Yield: 1 8x8-inch pan

- ½ cup oil
- ½ cup applesauce
- ¾ cup sugar
- 1 large egg
- 1 ½ cups flour
- 1 teaspoon baking powder
- 1 teaspoon cinnamon
- ¼ teaspoon nutmeg
- ¼ teaspoon salt

1. Preheat oven to 350° F. and grease pan.

2. Mix oil, applesauce, sugar, and egg in a medium bowl. Stir in flour, baking powder, cinnamon, nutmeg, and salt.

3. Pour into prepared pan and bake 30 to 35 minutes, until the top feels firm when gently pressed and the blondie pulls away from the sides of the pan.

4. Keeps two days at room temperature. For longer storage keep in fridge.

INSIDER TIPS
- Quick fix
- Add 1 cup chopped or grated apples in season.
- Top with spiced buttercream frosting (Chapter 15).

CATEGORIES
- Nut free

Toffee Butterscotch Blondies

These are in the ooey-gooey category.

Yield: 1 8x8-inch pan

- 6 ounces (1 ½ sticks) butter, melted
- 1 ½ cups brown sugar
- 1 large egg
- 1 teaspoon vanilla
- 1 ½ cups flour
- ½ teaspoon baking powder
- ¼ teaspoon salt
- 1 (8-ounce) bag toffee bits, approximately 1 ⅓ cups

1. Preheat oven to 350° F. and grease pan.

2. Mix together butter and brown sugar in a medium bowl. Cool for a few minutes. Add egg and vanilla and mix well. Add the flour, baking powder, and salt, combining until there are no more lumps of flour. Mix in 1 cup of toffee bits, reserving ⅓ cup for topping. The batter will be thick.

3. Scoop into prepared pan and spread evenly into all corners. Sprinkle on remaining toffee bits.

4. Bake 35 to 45 minutes, until the blondies are golden brown and pull away from the sides of the pan. Keeps up to five days at room temperature.

INSIDER TIPS
- Quick fix

CATEGORIES
- Nut free

Walnut Blondies

A fast and versatile dough. This is my basic recipe for blonde brownies. Make them with nuts, chocolate chips, or any addition your customers like.

Yield: 1 9x13-inch pan

- 6 ounces (1 ½ sticks) butter, melted
- 2 cups brown sugar
- 3 large eggs
- 1 tablespoon vanilla
- 2 ¼ cups flour
- 2 teaspoons baking powder
- 1 teaspoon salt
- 1 ½ cups chopped walnuts

1. Preheat oven to 350° F. and grease pan.

2. Mix together butter and brown sugar in a medium bowl. Cool for a few minutes. Mix in eggs and vanilla. Add flour, baking powder, and salt, mixing until there are no more lumps of flour. Mix in nuts. The batter will be thick.

3. Scoop into the prepared pan and spread evenly into all corners.

4. Bake 35 to 45 minutes, until the blondies are a golden brown and pull away from the sides of the pan. Keeps five days at room temperature.

INSIDER TIPS
- Quick fix
- Add 1 cup chocolate chips.
- Substitute pecans for walnuts.
- Stir in red and green candies during the winter holiday season.
- Reserve ½ cup nuts from recipe and sprinkle on before baking.

Chapter 7

Coffeecakes

Coffeecakes are such a great seller that they deserve their own chapter. I've included a variety of recipes, some with butter and some with oil (oil-based recipes are the easiest and fastest to whip up), some whole grain, some with only white flour, and some that work well with seasonal fruit.

If coffeecakes will be part of your regular product line, make a large batch of any streusel topping and keep it in the fridge for ease of production. If you have a good basic sweetbread (loaf) recipe you already like, try making it into a coffeecake with fruit, then add a topping.

People seem more willing to eat a good-for-you whole wheat coffeecake when it's associated with breakfast. So customers who eat coffeecakes for brunch or breakfast, as opposed to an afternoon snack, are more accepting of baked goods made with whole grain flour. Know your target market. This is not a scientific study, just an opinion culled from personal market research studies and from knowing my target market.

Tips for baking:
- Add extra flour when adding extra fresh produce, approximately ¼ cup flour for 1 additional cup produce. The flour helps offset the additional moisture.

Tips for handling:
- After baking, refrigerate coffeecakes with lots of fresh produce. Otherwise they can mold quickly, especially in warm weather.

- Sometimes a coating of confectioners' sugar dissolves into the product after several hours. This depends upon how you bake and store items, and relates to ambient temperature and moisture levels. Simply freshen with more sugar and re-wrap for sale.

Variations:
- All recipes can be baked as muffins.

- Add a streusel topping or sprinkling of sugar before baking. Raw sugar looks especially attractive because of its larger crystals.

- After baking, finish any coffeecake with confectioners' sugar, glaze, or string icing (Chapter 15).

- Coffeecakes are especially adaptable to seasonal produce.

- Sell in paper or aluminum pans and package with a plastic knife.

- For pie-shaped pans, place fruit in bottom of pie pan, pour batter over fruit, add topping, bake, and finish. This method only works if coffeecake is sold in the pan.

- Bake in springform pans and sell by wedges.

- Bake in sheet pans and cut extra big pieces. Overwrap each piece and stack high on a display tray within reach of customers. Put a sign in front of the stack with the product name, price, and that it's "breakfast for one."

Zak's early spring garden inspired Pretty in Pink Rhubarb Coffeecake.

Apple Date Coffeecake

This coffeecake began as a gingerbread cake then took a permanent detour when I accidentally mixed in dates that had been soaking for another recipe. I put it out for samples and customers fell in love. It's nourishing without tasting healthy.

Yield: 1 8x8-inch pan

- 1 cup chopped dates
- ¾ cup hot coffee (or any hot liquid)
- ¼ cup oil
- 1 large egg
- ½ cup sugar
- ¼ cup molasses
- 1 teaspoon vanilla
- 1 ½ cups whole wheat pastry flour
- 1 teaspoon baking soda
- 1 teaspoon ground ginger
- ¼ teaspoon salt
- 1 medium apple, chopped, with skin
- confectioners' sugar for top of cake, optional

1. Soak dates in hot coffee for at least 30 minutes.

2. Preheat oven to 350° F. and grease pan.

3. Combine oil, egg, sugar, molasses, and vanilla in a medium bowl. Add dates and liquid and stir. Combine flour, baking soda, ginger, and salt in a separate bowl. Mix into the wet ingredients. Stir in the apples. The batter will be thick.

4. Pour into the prepared pan and bake 30 to 35 minutes, until the cake pulls away from sides of pan and the cake top feels firm. Keeps several days at room temperature, or one week in the fridge.

INSIDER TIPS
- Quick fix
- For seasonal changes, use pears in fall, plums in summer.
- Sprinkle with streusel before baking.

CATEGORIES
- Whole grain
- Dairy free
- Nut free

Cinnamon Crumb Topped Coffeecake

Pay attention to these instructions! The process is a bit different but if you're looking for a moist coffeecake with a cinnamon streusel, the results are worth the effort.

Yield: 1 8x8-inch pan

- 1 ½ cups sugar
- 2 ¼ cups flour
- ¼ teaspoon salt
- ½ cup shortening
- 6 tablespoons (¾ stick) butter, divided
- 1 ½ teaspoons cinnamon
- 1 large egg
- ¼ cup milk
- 1 teaspoon vanilla
- ¼ cup flour
- 1 teaspoon baking powder

1. Preheat oven to 350° F. and grease pan.

2. Stir together sugar, flour, and salt in a large bowl. Cut in the shortening and ¼ cup (½ stick) of butter until the fat resembles pea-sized pieces.

3. Put 2 ½ cups of this mixture into another bowl and stir in cinnamon. Cut in the last 2 tablespoons (¼ stick) butter and set aside. This will be the streusel crumb topping.

4. Add the egg, milk, vanilla, flour, and baking powder to the first bowl. Beat until thoroughly combined.

5. Pour batter into prepared pan. Sprinkle streusel on top.

6. Bake 35 to 45 minutes, until a toothpick inserted into the center comes out dry and the top feels firm when gently pressed. Keeps several days at room temperature.

INSIDER TIPS
- Add raisins or chopped dates to batter.
- Add mini-chocolate chips to crumb topping.
- After baking sift a thick layer of confectioners' sugar over the top.

CATEGORIES
- Nut free

Cinnamon Streusel Coffeecake

Here's a classic sour cream coffeecake with a swirl in every slice. It's one of my bestselling brunch cakes. We had orders every weekend for these moist cakes with a surprise nut and chocolate chip filling.

Yield: 1 12-cup tube pan

Filling

- ¼ cup brown sugar
- 1 ½ teaspoons cinnamon
- 1 tablespoon cocoa
- ¼ cup finely chopped nuts
- ¼ cup mini-chocolate chips or finely chopped chocolate

Cake

- 6 ounces (1 ½ sticks) butter
- 1 ½ cups sugar
- 3 large eggs
- 2 teaspoons vanilla
- 1 cup sour cream
- ½ cup milk
- 4 cups flour
- 1 ½ teaspoons baking soda
- 1 teaspoon baking powder
- ½ teaspoon salt

1. Preheat oven to 350° F. and grease baking pan.

2. Stir together all filling ingredients in a small bowl. Set aside.

3. Beat the butter, sugar, eggs, vanilla, and sour cream in a large bowl. Stir in milk.

4. Mix together flour, baking soda, baking powder, and salt in a separate large bowl. Add to the butter mixture, and beat until thoroughly mixed.

5. Pour approximately two-thirds of batter into the prepared pan. Evenly sprinkle on the filling, reserving 1 tablespoon. Add remaining batter and smooth the top. Sprinkle the last tablespoon of filling over the cake top.

6. Bake 55 to 65 minutes. The cake is done when a toothpick inserted into the center comes out dry, or the top feels firm when lightly pressed. Keeps several days at room temperature.

INSIDER TIPS

- Bake in a springform pan.
- Add 1 cup finely chopped seasonal fresh fruit such as apples or plums.

Danish Apple Walnut Cake

When I was a kid my mom made this for Sunday brunches. It was simple, moist, and delicious, but the top was quite unattractive. (Sorry mom.) Customers eat with their eyes first, so when I developed the bakery version I added streusel from another recipe. What a difference! This coffeecake became a permanent part of my product line. (Thanks mom.)

Yield: 1 8x8-inch pan

Streusel

- $^2/_3$ cup whole wheat pastry flour
- $^2/_3$ cup all-purpose flour
- $^2/_3$ cup sugar
- ½ teaspoon salt
- ½ teaspoon cinnamon
- $^1/_3$ cup oil
- 2 tablespoons water
- $^2/_3$ cup chopped walnuts, optional

Cake

- ¾ cup sugar
- $^1/_3$ cup oil
- 1 large egg
- 2 tablespoons apple or orange juice
- 1 teaspoon vanilla
- 1 ¾ cups flour
- 1 teaspoon baking soda
- 2 teaspoons cinnamon
- ¼ teaspoon salt
- 2 cups (2 medium) chopped apples, with skin
- ½ cup chopped walnuts

1. To make the streusel, mix both flours, sugar, salt, and cinnamon in a small bowl. Pour in the oil and water, and combine thoroughly. Set aside.

2. Preheat oven to 350° F. and grease pan.

3. To make the cake, combine sugar, oil, egg, juice, and vanilla in a large bowl.

4. Stir together the flour, baking soda, cinnamon, and salt in a medium bowl. Mix into wet ingredients. Stir in apples and nuts. The batter will be thick.

5. Pour into baking pan, sprinkle on streusel, and bake 40 to 50 minutes, until the top feels firm and a toothpick inserted in the center comes out dry. Save any unused streusel for other products. Keeps one week at room temperature, two weeks if refrigerated.

INSIDER TIPS

- If you will be using streusel regularly, make a large batch.
- This recipe adapts well to most seasonal fruits, especially pears, plums, or peaches.
- Makes a nice apple cake. Do not use streusel, frost with vanilla or spiced buttercream (Chapter 15).
- This coffeecake is not Danish in origin and not related to Danish pastry. During recipe development, we tossed around several names and this one stuck. Name it anything that sounds appealing.
- Of course, nuts may be left out.

CATEGORIES

- Dairy free

Gingerbread Pear Coffeecake

This coffeecake is made with all whole wheat flour and sweetened only with molasses. It sold well during the fall and winter seasons.

Yield: 1 8x8-inch pan

- ¼ cup oil
- ½ cup molasses
- 1 large egg
- 1 teaspoon vanilla
- ½ cup buttermilk
- 1 ¾ cups whole wheat pastry flour
- 1 ½ teaspoons ground ginger
- 1 ½ teaspoons cinnamon
- ¾ teaspoon baking soda
- ¼ teaspoon salt
- 1-2 medium pears, chopped, with skin

1. Preheat oven to 350° F. and grease pan.

2. Mix together oil, molasses, egg, and vanilla in a medium bowl. Stir in buttermilk.

3. Combine flour, ginger, cinnamon, baking soda, and salt in another bowl. Stir into the molasses mixture. Then stir in pear(s). The batter should be thick.

4. Pour into prepared pan and bake 30 to 40 minutes, until the cake begins to pull away from the sides of the pan and the top feels firm when gently pressed. Keeps several days at room temperature or refrigerate for longer storage.

INSIDER TIPS
- Quick fix
- Substitute apples for pears.
- This recipe looks nice with a plain glaze (Chapter 15).
- Promote the no-white-sugar aspect (but no glaze allowed if you do!)

CATEGORIES
- Whole grain
- Nut free

Gingerbread Cake

This simple coffeecake has extra flavor from fresh grated ginger. It always got a special "wow" from customers.

Yield: 1 8x8-inch pan

- ½ cup oil
- ¼ cup molasses
- ½ cup sugar
- 2 large eggs
- 2 teaspoons vanilla
- 1 cup buttermilk
- 2 ½ cups flour
- 2 teaspoons baking soda
- ½ teaspoon salt
- 2 teaspoons ground ginger
- 1 teaspoon cinnamon
- ¼ teaspoon cloves
- 2 tablespoons fresh grated ginger
- ½ cup chopped crystallized ginger, optional

1. Preheat oven to 350° F. and grease pan.

2. Beat together oil, molasses, sugar, eggs, vanilla, and buttermilk in a medium bowl.

3. Mix the flour, baking soda, salt, ginger, cinnamon, and cloves in a separate bowl. Stir into the wet ingredients until there are no lumps. Add the fresh ginger and crystallized ginger, if using.

4. Pour into prepared pan and bake 25 to 35 minutes, until a toothpick inserted in the center comes out clean and the cake feels firm when gently pressed. Keeps several days.

INSIDER TIPS
- Quick fix

CATEGORIES
- Nut free

Hummingbird Coffeecake

The name Hummingbird refers to a moist cake of southern origin. The ingredients usually include chopped bananas, crushed pineapple, pecans, and coconut. But chopped bananas can turn an unsightly brown so I developed this recipe based on one of my banana cake recipes.

Yield: 1 8x8-inch pan

- ½ cup oil
- 1 cup sugar
- 1 large egg
- 1 cup (2 small) mashed bananas
- 1 teaspoon vanilla
- 2 cups flour
- ½ teaspoon baking soda
- ½ teaspoon baking powder
- 1 teaspoon cinnamon
- ¼ teaspoon salt
- ¾ cup sweetened coconut
- 1 (8-ounce) can crushed pineapple, undrained
- ½ cup chopped pecans, optional

1. Preheat oven to 350° F. and grease pan.

2. Beat together oil, sugar, egg, bananas, and vanilla in a medium bowl.

3. Stir together flour, baking soda, baking powder, cinnamon, and salt in a separate bowl. Mix into the liquid ingredients. Add coconut, pineapple, and nuts, if using. Mix well.

4. Pour into prepared pan and bake 35 to 45 minutes, until the top feels firm when gently pressed and a toothpick inserted near the center comes out clean. Refrigerate if keeping more than two days.

INSIDER TIPS
- Quick fix
- Add a streusel or glaze (Chapter 15).

CATEGORIES
- Dairy free

Jam Swirled Coffeecake

After baking, add confectioners' sugar. It soaks through to the jam for an attractive appearance.

Yield: 1 8x8-inch pan

- 6 ounces (1 ½ sticks) butter
- 1 ¹/₃ cups sugar
- 2 large eggs
- 2 teaspoons vanilla
- ²/₃ cup milk
- 2 ¼ cups flour
- 2 teaspoons baking powder
- ¼ teaspoon salt
- ½ cup fruit jam, any variety

1. Preheat oven to 350° F. and grease baking pan.

2. Beat together butter, sugar, eggs, and vanilla in a medium bowl. Stir in milk.

3. Mix together flour, baking powder, and salt in a separate bowl. Add to the butter mixture. Beat until thoroughly mixed.

4. Spread batter into prepared pan. Drop several tablespoons of jam over the cake, evenly spaced. Use a toothpick or sharp knife to pull through jam, creating swirls.

5. Bake 40 to 50 minutes until cake turns a medium golden brown.

6. Cool and finish with a thick dusting of confectioners' sugar. Keeps several days at room temperature.

INSIDER TIPS
- Quick fix
- Best selling flavors are apricot, raspberry, and strawberry.
- For Blueberry Apricot Coffeecake, use apricot jam and sprinkle with 1 cup blueberries. Press blueberries lightly into batter and top with 2 tablespoons granulated sugar.

CATEGORIES
- Nut free

Lemon Blueberry Coffeecake

One of the best coffeecakes ever! We sold these cut into huge slabs and wrapped for "single-serving" size. The message? "Eat this all by yourself."

Yield: 1 9x9-inch pan

- ¼ pound (1 stick) butter
- 1 ½ cups sugar
- 1 large egg
- 1 teaspoon lemon extract
- ½ teaspoon vanilla extract
- ½ cup sour cream
- ½ cup milk
- 3 ¼ cups flour
- 1 teaspoon baking powder
- ½ teaspoon baking soda
- ½ teaspoon salt
- 2 cups fresh or fresh frozen blueberries (do not thaw)

1. Preheat oven to 350° F. and grease pan.

2. Cream butter and sugar in a medium bowl. Add the egg, extracts, sour cream, and milk and stir well to combine. This mixture might look curdled but that's okay.

3. Beat in the flour, baking powder, baking soda, and salt until all the flour is incorporated. You'll have a lot of batter, which makes a thick coffeecake.

4. Pour batter into prepared pan and sprinkle blueberries evenly over the top. Do not press in. Most will fall while baking and some may stay near the top for nice visibility.

5. Bake 45 to 60 minutes, until the top feels firm when gently pressed and a toothpick inserted in the center comes out clean. Keeps two or three days at room temperature.

INSIDER TIPS
- Bake in a springform pan; top with streusel.
- For seasonal changes, use chopped fresh summer fruits such as peaches or plums.
- Sprinkle before baking with granulated or raw sugar, or finish after baking with confectioners' sugar or string icing (Chapter 15).

CATEGORIES
- Nut free

Pretty in Pink Rhubarb Coffeecake

This oil-based coffeecake is fast to whip up and good with any seasonal fruit. I developed this recipe for rhubarb, the first sign of spring, then used it throughout the spring and summer seasons adding whatever local fruit was available.

Yield: 1 8x8-inch pan

- ½ cup vegetable oil
- ¾ cup sugar
- 1 large egg
- 1 teaspoon vanilla
- ½ cup buttermilk
- 2 cups flour
- ½ teaspoon baking soda
- ½ teaspoon salt
- 2 cups chopped fruit

1. Preheat oven to 350° F. and grease pan.

2. Combine oil, sugar, egg, vanilla, and buttermilk in a medium bowl.

3. Stir together flour, baking soda, and salt in a separate medium bowl. Add to the liquid ingredients.

4. Stir in fruit and pour into the prepared pan. If using frozen fruit, do not thaw or mix in with batter, just sprinkle fruit evenly over batter and lightly press.

5. Bake 30 to 40 minutes, until the top feels firm when gently pressed or a toothpick inserted near center comes out clean. Keeps several days or refrigerate for longer storage.

INSIDER TIPS
- Quick fix
- Sprinkle with raw sugar or streusel (Chapter 15) before baking.
- Also good using dried fruits, particularly apricots or cranberries.

CATEGORIES
- Nut free

Sweet Potato Pecan Coffeecake

This coffeecake sells well throughout the fall and winter but does exceptionally well during the days leading up to Thanksgiving.

Yield: 1 8x8-inch pan

- ¾ cup oil
- ½ cup sugar
- ½ cup brown sugar
- 2 large eggs
- 1 teaspoon vanilla
- 1 cup mashed sweet potatoes, fresh or canned
- 1 tablespoon fresh grated ginger
- 2 cups flour
- 1 teaspoon baking soda
- 1 ½ teaspoons cinnamon
- ½ teaspoon ground ginger
- ¼ teaspoon salt
- 1 cup chopped pecans

1. Preheat oven to 350° F. and grease pan.

2. Combine oil, both sugars, eggs, and vanilla in a medium bowl. Stir in sweet potatoes and fresh grated ginger.

3. Stir together flour, baking soda, cinnamon, ground ginger, and salt in a separate bowl. Add to wet ingredients and mix well. Stir in half the pecans, reserving half for sprinkling on top after panning.

4. Pour batter into the prepared pan and top with remaining pecans.

5. Bake 40 to 50 minutes, until the top feels firm when gently pressed, or a toothpick inserted near the center comes out clean. Keeps several days at room temperature.

INSIDER TIPS
- Leave out the fresh ginger and add 1 teaspoon additional ground ginger, but fresh makes a remarkable taste difference.
- When cool, top with confectioners' sugar.
- Top with streusel or string icing (Chapter 15).

CATEGORIES
- Dairy free

Chapter 8

Cookies! Cookies! Cookies!

In both my home business and retail bakery, we had a few classic flavors of cookies which were perennial best sellers, plus some unique recipes that proved popular. Some became a permanent part of my product line while others, to keep interest high, were rotated flavors.

Some cookie types have a specific customer purpose. Customers order them for special occasions such as social gatherings, meetings, or (as with holiday cookies) gifting. Most cookies, however, are an impulse purchase. Customers rarely drive across town for a cookie. Someone happens to be near a cookie and thinks, "Oh, I'm hungry," and reaches for something to eat. Keep this in mind when you're deciding which ones to bake for retail sales at farmers' markets. Make a limited number of short shelf life cookies and fill in with varieties that can last until you're back at the market the following week.

Consider using scoops for consistent size, if you don't already use them. See portion control/scoop chart at end of book. Small cookies are a tablespoon of dough and large cookies are 3-4 tablespoons. For large cookies I use scoop 20, which holds approximately 3 tablespoons.

Tips for baking:

- For easy clean-up, line cookie sheets with foil, silicone mats, or parchment paper. After each use, wipe down with a clean paper or cloth towel. Liners can be used multiple times.

- All recipes may be baked as large or small cookies.

- When making small cookies, I don't use a very small scoop. Doing so can be incredibly tedious, especially for anyone prone to repetitive task injury. I use a large scoop to portion all the dough, placing the balls close together on a cookie sheet. Then by hand I divide the balls into thirds or quarters. Each ball is not exactly the same size, but they're close enough and it's easier on your hands.

- If your drop cookie dough is sticky and difficult to work with, place a small bowl of water nearby. Occasionally dip your fingers or the scoop into the water and continue. The extra water shouldn't hurt your end product.

- Customers like value for their money. Consider flattening cookie dough before baking so the finished product appears larger.

- You may refrigerate drop cookie doughs (except meringues) before baking. Scoop out all the dough right after mixing. Place close together on a tray, cover and chill, then use as needed. Doughs keep at least one week if well-wrapped.

- Rolled cookies may be baked as drop cookies and vice versa.

Tips for handling:
- To store soft cookies after baking, place waxed paper or parchment sheets between layers.

- Cookie cutters can be cute, but those with solid tops are difficult for removing dough. Cutters with appendages break easily.

- For dipping cookies: use real chocolate (which must be tempered) or faux chocolate coverings (wafers or melts), which do not need to be tempered. I often use a combination of the two. I simply melt the wafers, then add real chocolate and stir.

Variations:
- Experiment! Try making any of these cookies as a bar cookie. Or use the cookie dough as a crust. Bake or par bake, then spread with jam or a brownie batter and bake until done.

- Many of these recipes work as small sandwich cookies. Bake small drop cookies, sandwich with jam, and dip part-way in chocolate. Add sprinkles for a festive appearance. For large trays, I use a different sprinkle color with each flavor of jam.

- Chocolate chip cookies using semi-sweet chocolate chips are the standard (and number one) seller. But there are many bits and chip varieties. Make variations based on customer interest.

- All cookies may be wrapped and sold individually or several in a package.

Sweet Shortbread Cut-Outs

Bakery Sprinkle Cookies

These are the large sugar cookies sold in retail bakeries. Many customers just like a plain sugar cookie.

Yield: 20 large or 60 small cookies

- ¼ pound (1 stick) butter
- ½ cup vegetable shortening
- 2 cups sugar
- 2 large eggs
- 2 teaspoons vanilla extract
- ½ teaspoon lemon or orange extract
- 3 ¾ cups flour
- 2 teaspoons baking powder
- ½ teaspoon baking soda
- 1 teaspoon salt
- sprinkles for topping

1. Preheat oven to 350° F. and prepare cookie sheets with liners.

2. Beat butter, shortening, and sugar in a large bowl. Add eggs and extracts, beating well until thoroughly combined. Mix in flour, baking powder, baking soda, and salt.

3. Scoop into equal-sized balls, approx ¼ cup. Flatten slightly for a larger appearance or leave as a ball for chewier cookies. Top with sprinkles before baking.

4. Bake 14 to 15 minutes depending upon thickness of cookie. Remove from oven when the top appears dry with moistness showing through the cracks. Bake longer for crispy cookies. Keeps at room temperature at least one week.

INSIDER TIPS
- For classic Snickerdoodles, omit citrus extract and roll dough in cinnamon sugar before baking.
- After cookies cool, glaze (Chapter 15) and add sprinkles.

CATEGORIES
- Nut free

Chinese Almond Cookies

These are a classic version of those large crumbly-chewy shortbread cookies sold in retail baker-ies. For an extra crunch, substitute a half cup almond meal for a half cup of flour. For a traditional bakery look, top with an almond.

Yield: 30-36 large cookies

- ½ pound (2 sticks) butter
- 1 cup vegetable shortening
- 2 cups sugar
- 1 large egg
- 1 tablespoon almond extract
- 4 cups flour
- ½ teaspoon salt
- ½ teaspoon baking soda
- 30-36 large whole almonds, optional

1. Preheat oven to 350° F. and prepare cookie sheets with liners.

2. Cream butter, shortening, and sugar in a large bowl. Add egg and extract, and beat until combined. Mix in flour, salt, and baking soda. The dough will be very stiff.

3. Scoop into equal-sized balls, approximately ¼ cup, and drop onto prepared cookie sheets. Press down slightly. If using whole almonds, place one in center of each cookie.

4. Bake 12 to 15 minutes. For a softer, chewy cookie, they should look slightly wet in the center. For a crisper, crumblier cookie, bake until the edges are a golden brown. Centers should remain white. Cookies keep at least two weeks.

INSIDER TIPS
- Hand-shape these cookies into forms such as hearts or stars.
- Add 2 cups chocolate chips, chopped almonds, or cinnamon hearts.

Chocolate and Spice Rolled Cookies

Before Christmas one year, baker Saraly suggested we make a chocolate version of her ginger-bread cookies. It sounded weird to me but I mixed a batch of dark spiced chocolate dough based on her original recipe. She cut them into teddy bears and after baking we piped on cute faces with holly-berry collars. These became a year-round winner (with proper seasonal collars)!

Yield: 36-48 cookies, assorted shapes and sizes

- ½ pound (2 sticks) butter
- 1 cup sugar
- ⅔ cup molasses
- 1 large egg
- ½ teaspoon vanilla
- 3 cups flour, plus more for rolling
- 1 ¼ cups cocoa
- 1 teaspoon baking soda
- 1 ½ teaspoons ginger
- 1 ½ teaspoons cinnamon
- ¼ teaspoon salt

1. Cream butter and sugar in a large bowl. Add molasses, egg, and vanilla, and cream until thoroughly combined.

2. In a separate bowl stir together the flour, cocoa, baking soda, ginger, cinnamon, and salt. Add to the wet ingredients and mix until all the dry is incorporated. The dough should be very stiff. If it's sticky, add more flour.

3. Divide into two pieces, wrap each, and refrigerate until hard. The dough keeps for up to two weeks in the fridge.

4. When ready to bake, preheat oven to 350° F. Prepare pans with liners and remove dough from refrigerator.

5. When dough is slightly soft and ready to roll out (five or ten minutes), sprinkle more flour on both the top and bottom of the dough. Roll ⅛- to ¼-inch thick, flouring as needed so the dough doesn't stick to the counter or rolling pin. Cut into teddy bears or any shape you prefer. Place at least 1-inch apart on baking sheets.

6. Bake 12 to 18 minutes, until a finger pressed lightly into the cookie leaves no imprint. Bake longer for crunchier cookies, but watch carefully. Cocoa makes it hard to see the darkening edges. Cool before decorating. Cookies keep for one month.

INSIDER TIPS

- For any holiday, bake assorted shapes and package for sale by the dozen. Tie bag with a large decorative ribbon.
- Instead of rolling out dough, bake as drop cookies. Scoop into equal-sized balls, place two inches apart on cookie sheet, and bake using time and temperature above.

CATEGORIES

- Nut free

Chocolate Oatmeal Cookies

These are dark, moist, chocolaty oatmeal cookies. Dipping in white chocolate makes an exceptionally tasty and unusual variation.

Yield: 24 medium or 48 small cookies

- ¼ pound (1 stick) butter
- ½ cup vegetable shortening
- 1 cup brown sugar
- ½ cup granulated sugar
- 2 large eggs
- 2 teaspoons vanilla
- 1 ½ cups flour
- ½ cup cocoa
- 1 teaspoon baking soda
- ½ teaspoon salt
- 3 cups rolled oats
- 1 cup chocolate chips, optional
- ½ cup chopped nuts, optional
- white chocolate for dipping, optional

1. Preheat oven to 350° F. and prepare cookie sheets with liners.

2. Cream butter, shortening, and both sugars in a large bowl. Mix in eggs and vanilla.

3. Add flour, cocoa, baking soda, salt, and oats, mixing well. The dough should be stiff. Stir in the chocolate chips and nuts, if using.

4. Drop tablespoons of dough onto lined cookie sheets, leaving at least two inches between them. Press down slightly. If the dough is a little sticky, wet fingertips before pressing.

5. Bake until almost set, 10 to 15 minutes, depending upon size. Cocoa makes it hard to see the darkening edges so watch closely and be careful not to over-bake.

6. If finishing with white chocolate, melt chocolate and dip cooled cookies half-way. Let harden before wrapping or storing. Cookies keep for several days.

INSIDER TIPS
- For storage, place wax paper between layers.
- Make into sandwich cookies using a jam or buttercream filling.

Cinnamon or Chocolate Marble Cookies

These thick and chewy cookies come with a wallop of cinnamon. I'd seen a magazine picture and decided to create my own. They became an instant hit with my customers, who then asked for a chocolate version.

Yield: 24 large cookies

- ¼ pound (1 stick) butter
- ½ cup vegetable shortening
- 2 cups brown sugar
- 2 large eggs
- 1 tablespoon vanilla
- 4 cups flour
- 1½ teaspoons baking powder
- ¾ teaspoon baking soda
- 1 teaspoon salt
- 1½ tablespoons cinnamon for cinnamon marble *or* 2 tablespoons vegetable oil mixed with ¼ cup cocoa for chocolate marble

1. Preheat oven to 350° F. and prepare cookie sheets with liners.

2. Beat together butter, shortening, and sugar in a large bowl. Add eggs and vanilla beating until thoroughly combined.

3. Mix in flour, baking powder, baking soda, and salt. The dough will be stiff.

4. Remove half the dough from bowl. For cinnamon marble, thoroughly blend cinnamon with remaining dough. For chocolate marble, mix in the oil-cocoa mixture until well combined. Barely mix the flavored dough with the plain dough. If you mix too much, the marbled effect will be lost.

5. For large cookies, scoop into equal-sized balls using approximately ¼ cup dough. Either flatten slightly for a larger appearance or leave as a ball for thicker, chewier cookies.

6. Bake 12 to15 minutes. Remove from oven when tops appear dry with moistness showing through the cracks. Bake longer for crisp, dry cookies. Keeps at least one week at room temperature.

INSIDER TIPS

- For Chocolate Mint Marble cookies, add ¼ teaspoon mint extract to chocolate dough.
- For Double Chocolate Marble cookies, add ½ cup mini-chocolate chips to chocolate dough.
- Bake as small cookies for an unusual addition to cookie trays.

CATEGORIES

- Nut free

Classic Honey Graham Crackers

Crisp and not too sweet, these grahams are one hundred percent whole grain, with honey instead of sugar.

Yield: 24-36 graham crackers

- ¼ pound (1 stick) butter
- ¼ cup honey
- 2 teaspoons vanilla
- ¼ cup water
- 2 cups whole wheat pastry flour
- 1 teaspoon baking powder
- ½ teaspoon baking soda
- 1 teaspoon cinnamon
- $^1/_8$ teaspoon salt
- raw sugar for topping, optional

1. Preheat oven to 350° F. and prepare cookie sheets with liners.

2. Cream butter with honey in a medium bowl. Blend in vanilla and water.

3. In a separate bowl stir together flour, baking powder, baking soda, cinnamon, and salt. Add to the butter mixture and combine thoroughly. Using your hand, push dough around the bowl until all flour is incorporated. The dough will be very dense.

4. Lightly flour your workspace and place the dough on top. Press down and shape into a rectangle. Flour top of the dough and roll to approximately $^1/_8$-inch thick.

5. Cut into squares using a pastry cutter, pizza cutter, or sharp knife. For a traditional graham cracker look, prick each cracker several times with a fork.

6. Transfer to the prepared cookie sheets, leaving at least 1-inch between cookies. If desired, sprinkle with raw sugar.

7. Bake 25 to 30 minutes, until slightly darker around the edges. Keeps up to six weeks in tightly covered containers.

INSIDER TIPS

- For vegan graham crackers, substitute margarine for butter, and ¼ cup sugar for honey. Add 2 tablespoons water.
- Use cookie cutters to make graham cracker shapes.

CATEGORIES

- Whole grain
- Egg free
- Nut free

Double Gingersnaps

These spicy ginger cookies with an extra hit of ginger are one hundred percent whole grain.

Yield: 12 large or 36 small cookies

- ¾ cup vegetable oil
- 1 cup sugar
- ¼ cup molasses
- 1 large egg
- ½ teaspoon vanilla
- 2 tablespoons grated fresh ginger
- 2 ¼ cups whole wheat pastry flour
- 1½ teaspoons baking soda
- 2 teaspoons cinnamon
- 2 teaspoons ground ginger
- ½ teaspoon cloves
- ¼ teaspoon nutmeg
- ¼ teaspoon salt
- granulated or raw sugar, for rolling

1. Preheat oven to 350° F. and prepare cookie sheets with liners.

2. In a large bowl mix together oil, sugar, molasses, egg, vanilla, and grated ginger.

3. In a separate bowl stir together flour, baking soda, spices, and salt. Add to the wet ingredients, mixing well.

4. Roll equal-sized balls of dough in sugar and place on cookie sheets at least two inches apart. Bake 10 to15 minutes depending upon size, until the tops appear set and the sides are slightly browner than the center dough. Tops of the cookies will feel dry to the touch. Bake less and they will be chewy; bake more for that crisp "snap." These cookies have a long shelf life, at least one month.

INSIDER TIPS

- Add ½ cup chopped crystallized ginger.
- Add even more spice (start with an additional ½ teaspoon each cinnamon and ground ginger) for a super punch. Advertise these as having extra zing.
- Make small cookies and sandwich them together with a filling of ginger preserves.

CATEGORIES

- Whole grain
- Dairy free
- Nut free

Gold Star Chocolate Chip Cookies

Customers give these cookies a gold star for looks and flavor. A hint of maple extract is the secret ingredient creating a subtle richness and depth of flavor.

Yield: 36 large or 72 medium cookies

- ½ pound (2 sticks) butter
- 1 cup vegetable shortening
- 2 ½ cups brown sugar
- 1 large egg
- 1 tablespoon vanilla extract
- ½ teaspoon maple extract
- 4 cups flour
- 1 ½ teaspoons baking soda
- 1 teaspoon salt
- 3 cups (one 6-ounce and one 12-ounce bag) chocolate chips

1. Preheat oven 375° F. and prepare cookie sheets with liners.

2. In a large bowl cream butter and vegetable shortening with sugar. Add egg, vanilla and maple extracts, and cream well.

3. Mix in flour, baking soda, and salt; scrape bowl to incorporate all ingredients. Add chips and mix until evenly combined. The dough will be very stiff.

4. Drop dough at least 2-inches apart and bake 10 to 15 minutes, depending upon size. Cookies are done when the outside rim is golden brown and the top is a light brown. Center of cookies might look soft and wet, but they will continue to bake after they are out of the oven. Keeps two or three days at room temperature.

INSIDER TIPS
- Add 1 cup coconut, candy pieces, raisins, or dried cranberries.
- Bake cookies without chocolate chips. After cooling, dip partially in melted white or dark chocolate.
- Make cookie cakes. Use a full cup of dough, one cookie per sheet tray, flatten, and bake at 350° F for 20 to 25 minutes. Sandwich together with a chocolate filling and sell by the slice.

CATEGORIES
- Nut free

Lemon Butter Cut-Outs

These sturdy cut-out cookies, made with cream cheese and butter, were so tasty my customers never suspected they were whole grain.

Yield: 24-36 large cookies

- ½ pound (2 sticks) butter
- 3 ounces cream cheese, softened
- 1 cup sugar
- 1 large egg
- 1 tablespoon lemon juice
- 1 ½ teaspoons lemon extract
- 3 cups whole wheat pastry flour
- 1 cup all-purpose flour
- ¼ teaspoon salt

1. Preheat oven to 375 °F. and prepare cookie sheets with liners.

2. Cream butter, cream cheese, and sugar in a large bowl. Beat in the egg, lemon juice, and extract.

3. Mix in both flours and salt until evenly combined. Roll out the dough immediately or refrigerate for up to two weeks.

4. For rolling, flour the workspace and top of the dough. Roll approximately ⅛-inch thick and cut out shapes making sure all cookies are the same thickness.

5. Place 1-inch apart on cookie sheets and bake 7 to 12 minutes depending upon size. Cookies are done when edges are a medium golden brown. Cookies keep for three weeks.

INSIDER TIPS
- For holidays and events such as Valentine's Day, bake assorted shapes and bag for sale by the dozen. Tie with a large ribbon.
- Instead of rolling out dough, bake as drop cookies. Scoop into small equal-sized balls, place 2-inches apart on cookie sheet, and bake using time and temperature above.
- Make Lemon Sandwich Cookies. Spread with raspberry jam for filling.

CATEGORIES
- Whole grain
- Nut free

Meringue Drops

These tasty delicate drops are gluten-free and light in calories. Meringues can also be shaped as cups to hold fresh fruits or ice cream (there go the calories).

Yield: 12 medium cookies

- 3 large egg whites
- ¼ teaspoon cream of tartar
- ¾ cup sugar
- ½ teaspoon vanilla

1. Preheat oven to 250° F. and prepare cookie sheets with liners.

2. Put egg whites into a clean mixer and whip until peaks begin to form. Slowly add cream of tartar and sugar, then vanilla. Keep whipping until stiff.

3. Drop by spoonfuls onto a cookie sheet or use a pastry bag and tips to form stars.

4. Bake for 1 to 1 ½ hours until dry but not brown. If meringues begin to darken, drop oven temperature by 25° F.

5. Meringues are sensitive to humidity, so shelf life varies. They can keep for two weeks or only one day. Store in well-sealed containers with waxed paper between layers.

INSIDER TIPS
- Fold in colorful candy bits for the holidays, such as crushed peppermint sticks.
- For light chocolate meringues, sift 1 tablespoon cocoa into the sugar before whipping.
- Add ¼ cup mini chocolate chips or ½ cup shredded coconut.
- For meringue shells, pipe a 4-inch circle on the cookie sheet, fill in with more meringue, then pipe an edge around perimeter. Bake for about 2 hours, until dry.

CATEGORIES
- Dairy free
- Nut free
- Gluten free

Oatmeal Wedges

My customers adored these unusual, pie-shaped cookies which started as a back-of-the-box oatmeal recipe. Initially, I only made the wedges for catering; but after numerous requests I added them to the cookie rotation.

Yield: 24-48, varies depending upon size of wedges

- ½ pound (2 sticks) butter
- 1 ½ cups brown sugar
- 2 large eggs
- 2 teaspoons vanilla
- 2 cups flour
- 1 teaspoon baking soda
- 2 teaspoons cinnamon
- ½ teaspoon salt
- 3 cups oats (quick or old fashioned)
- approximately 1 cup melted chocolate

1. Preheat oven to 350° F. and prepare cookie sheets with liners.

2. Cream butter and sugar in a large bowl, then beat in eggs and vanilla.

3. Mix in flour, baking soda, cinnamon, and salt, until thoroughly combined. Add oats and mix well. The dough will be very stiff.

4. Measure dough. (After baking, every cookie will be cut into 8 pieces, so decide how large you want the final cookie wedge.) For small, delicate wedges, use ¼ cup dough. For larger cookies use 1 cup dough.

5. Drop onto prepared cookie sheets, then flatten slightly. Leave lots of room between the dough. For 1 cup dough you'll probably only bake 2 cookies per pan.

6. Bake 10 to 15 minutes, depending upon size of cookie. When done, edges will be light golden brown and the center will look a little soft and wet.

7. Let cookies cool for about 10 minutes. With a long sharp knife, press down and cut into eighths. Don't move the warm cookies or they might fall apart.

8. When cookies are cooled, melt semi-sweet chocolate or wafers and dip the cookie ends only. Let chocolate set before wrapping or storing. Keeps for several days in a cool location.

INSIDER TIPS

- After baking, store cookies without dipping, then dip later.
- For leftover chocolate, see recipe for Chocolate Medallions, Chapter 14.
- For mocha wedges, substitute 1 tablespoon coffee powder for cinnamon.

CATEGORIES

- Whole grain
- Nut free

Pfeffernuesse

My baker, Saraly, made "pepper nut" cookies rolled in powdered sugar. They're a traditional spiced German Christmas treat with a long shelf life, so you may start baking these at least a month before the holiday season begins.

Yield: 24-30 medium small cookies

- $1/8$ pound (½ stick) butter
- ¼ cup sugar
- 6 tablespoons molasses
- 1 large egg
- 1 tablespoon whiskey (or other liquor)
- 2 cups flour
- ½ teaspoon baking soda
- ¼ teaspoon salt
- ½ teaspoon cinnamon
- $1/8$ teaspoon cloves
- $1/8$ teaspoon nutmeg
- $1/8$ teaspoon finely ground black pepper
- confectioners' sugar for rolling

1. Preheat oven to 350° F. and prepare cookie sheets with liners.
2. Blend butter, sugar, molasses, egg, and whiskey in a large bowl until thoroughly combined. Mix in flour, baking soda, salt, cinnamon, cloves, nutmeg, and pepper. Dough will be very stiff and slightly sticky.
3. Scoop or pinch off tablespoons of dough and place at least 2-inches apart on cookie sheet. If dough is too sticky, periodically dip your fingers into a bowl of water. Extra water on the dough will not affect cookies.
4. Bake 10 to 12 minutes, depending upon size. Cookies are done when puffed and no imprint remains when gently pressed.
5. Cool thoroughly. Cookies can be rolled in confectioners' sugar before or after storing. Keeps several weeks in well-sealed containers.

INSIDER TIPS
- Bake small cookies for the holidays and large ones for year-round sales.
- Saraly's original recipe had twice the amount of spices. My customers preferred a milder cookie but your market research may have different results.

CATEGORIES
- Nut free

Sweet Shortbread Cut-Outs

Crisp and buttery, these cookies work well when the dough is colored for the holidays. Recipe, compliments of my baker, Saraly.

Yield: 36-48, depends upon size

- ½ pound (2 sticks) butter
- 1 cup confectioners' sugar
- 1 ½ teaspoons vanilla
- ¼ teaspoon salt
- 2 to 2 ¼ cups flour, plus more for rolling
- assorted food coloring, optional

1. Blend butter and sugar in a medium bowl, then mix in vanilla and salt. Add enough flour to make a stiff dough.

2. For plain dough, wrap in 2 or 3 separate disks. To color dough, divide into the number of different colors you desire and place each in a bowl. Mix each dough to the desired shade, shape into a flat disk, and wrap. Chill for several hours or up to two weeks.

3. When ready to bake, preheat oven to 375° F. and prepare cookie sheets with liners.

4. Let the discs of dough soften for a few minutes. Flour your work surface and the top of the dough and roll to an even thickness, approx ⅛- to ¼-inch thick. Cut into desired shapes and place close together on a cookie sheet. Don't let the dough sit too long or it will soften and become unmanageable. Re-wrap scraps and roll again.

5. Bake 8 to12 minutes, depending upon size of cookies. The edges should be light golden brown with no top browning. Keep in airtight container up to three weeks.

INSIDER TIPS

- For candy cane cookies, color half the dough red and hand shape into canes. Or be bold and use a variety of bright colors. I made many candy cane combinations (such as orange and pink, or blue and green) for decorating trays. Customers loved the unusual color combinations.
- For swirls, gently mix colored doughs together, and shape into logs. You may roll logs in sprinkles or colored sugar. Wrap, chill, slice, and bake.

- Use small cookie cutters such as hearts, leaves, people, or bells, and make several dozen of each shape in a variety of colors. Use to decorate cakes, cupcakes, and holiday trays.
- To make Poppy People, add 2 tablespoons poppy seeds with the flour and cut into people shapes.

CATEGORIES
- Egg free
- Nut free

Wine-Soaked Oatmeal Raisin Cookies

A customer (who shall remain nameless) loved oatmeal cookies. She assumed I wanted to know about each one she had ever eaten in the previous ten years, and how that cookie was not perfect. After I added these cookies made with wine-soaked raisins to our product line, she said, "You created these for me, because of my whining? How clever and nice. Don't I get them free?"

Yield: 12-24, depending upon size

- ½ cup red wine
- 1 ½ cups raisins
- ¼ pound (1 stick) butter
- 1 ½ cups brown sugar
- 1 large egg
- 1 teaspoon vanilla
- 2 cups flour
- ½ teaspoon baking powder
- ½ teaspoon baking soda
- 1 teaspoon cinnamon
- ½ teaspoon salt
- 1 ½ cups quick *or* rolled oats

1. At least one hour before preparing dough, soak raisins in wine. Stir occasionally.

2. Preheat oven to 375° F. and prepare cookie sheets with liners.

3. Cream butter, brown sugar, egg, and vanilla in a large bowl.

4. In another bowl mix, together flour, baking powder, baking soda, cinnamon, and salt. Add to the wet ingredients and mix until combined. Scrape bottom of the bowl several times.

5. Add oats, raisins, and wine, carefully folding in by hand. Once again, scrape the bottom of the bowl. The batter should be very stiff. Add more flour if necessary.

6. Drop dough in equal-sized pieces onto prepared trays. Flatten slightly and bake 12 to 15 minutes, or until lightly browned around edges. For a soft and chewy cookie, the center might look moist. Bake 2 to 3 minutes longer for a crisper cookie. Keeps several days.

INSIDER TIPS

- I prefer regular rolled oats because they're more visible after baking.
- Add ½ cup coconut or dried chopped apricots.
- These cookies are worth whining for, but if you don't want to use wine, substitute apple, orange, or grape juice.

CATEGORIES

- Whole grain
- Nut free

Chapter 9

Fruit Bars and Cookie Bars

For snack time, bars are customer favorites and are excellent sellers. They're quite easy to whip up. Many are simply cookies in disguise, but even those consisting of three levels (crust, filling, and topping) can take less time than baking individual cookies. Most are adaptable to seasonal variations. I wrote each recipe using its best selling fruit filling, but in the fall I often switch to apples and pears; and in the summer I use blueberries, raspberries, peaches, or nectarines. Use whatever seasonal produce you choose.

Raspberry Peach Custard Bars

Tips for Baking:

- If using frozen fruit, do not thaw before using, since most fruits don't hold their shape when they defrost.

- Bake bars in small disposable pans. Wrap well and tape plastic knife on top.

Tips for Handling:

- Most bars need to cool before cutting. If you are ever in doubt about pressing a knife through a cooled dense bar, score the top and resume cutting after it finishes cooling.

- Bars with a filling must always cool before cutting or the filling will ooze out.

- Sometimes bars have an unsightly, messy smear when cut. If this happens, dip knife in warm or hot water, wipe blade, and cut. You might have to dip before each cut. Or if you have time, refrigerate and cut while cold, or freeze for an hour or two.

Variations:

- Most bar recipes can be baked in round pans and presented as tarts.

- After baking, dust bars with confectioners' sugar.

- Add a string icing before cutting.

Blueberry Crumb Bars

These bars were originally part of my seasonal menu, but they were so popular I began making them year round. If using frozen fruits, do not let them thaw before using.

Yield: 1 8x8-inch pan

Crust and topping

- 3 cups flour
- 1 cup sugar
- ¼ teaspoon salt
- ½ pound (2 sticks) butter, melted

Filling

- 3 cups blueberries, fresh or frozen
- 1 tablespoon lemon juice
- 3 tablespoons sugar
- 1 tablespoon flour
- $^1/_8$ teaspoon cinnamon

1. Preheat oven to 350° F. and grease pan.

2. Stir together flour, sugar, salt, and melted butter in a medium bowl, until it begins to clump.

3. Reserve half the dough for the crumb topping. Firmly press the other half into bottom of pan. Bake 15 to 20 minutes, until light brown along edges. Let cool 5 minutes.

4. While crust is baking, mix together blueberries, lemon juice, sugar, flour, and cinnamon in a medium bowl. Spread over warm crust.

5. Sprinkle remaining crumbs over the blueberries and bake 40 to 50 minutes, until the top is a light golden brown and blueberry juice bubbles up the sides of pan. Keeps two days at room temperature, longer if refrigerated.

INSIDER TIPS
- Sprinkle with confectioners' sugar before cutting.
- Use any seasonal fruit, such as apples, peaches, or nectarines.

CATEGORIES
- Egg free
- Nut free

Cashew Sesame Honey Bars

These thick, yummy-looking treats stack well for display.

Yield: 1 8x8-inch pan

Crust

- ¼ pound (1 stick) butter
- ¼ cup confectioners' sugar
- 1 cup flour

Filling

- 2 large eggs
- ½ cup honey
- ½ cup sugar
- 2 tablespoons butter, melted
- 1 teaspoon vanilla
- $\frac{1}{8}$ teaspoon salt
- 1 ½ cups cashews, plain or salted
- 2 tablespoons sesame seeds

1. Preheat oven to 350° F. and lightly grease pan bottom and sides.

2. Cream butter, sugar, and flour in a medium bowl. Press into bottom of pan and bake 20 to 25 minutes until light golden brown. Cool 5 minutes.

3. While crust is baking, mix together eggs, honey, sugar, butter, vanilla, and salt in a medium bowl. Stir in cashews and sesame seeds.

4. When crust is cooled, pour filling on top and push nuts to evenly cover. Bake another 30 to 40 minutes, until filling is a light golden brown around edges and the top feels firm when gently pressed.

5. While still warm, run a knife between pan and edge of bars. Cool before cutting. Keeps one week in fridge.

INSIDER TIPS

- Add 1 cup (6-ounce bag) white chocolate chips and delete sesame seeds.
- Bake a three-nut honey bar using cashews, walnuts, and pecans.

Chocolate Chip Bar Cookies

A super quick fix when you don't have time to make cookies.

Yield: 1 10x15-inch jellyroll pan

- 6 ounces (1 ½ sticks) butter
- 1 ½ cups sugar
- ¼ cup corn syrup
- 2 teaspoons vanilla
- 3 large eggs
- 2 ¼ cups flour
- 2 ½ teaspoons baking powder
- 1 teaspoon salt
- 2 cups (12-ounce bag) chocolate chips

1. Preheat oven to 350° F. and grease pan.

2. Cream butter and sugar in large bowl, then mix in corn syrup, vanilla, and eggs.

3. Stir in flour, baking powder, and salt until thoroughly combined. Stir in chocolate chips.

4. Press into prepared pan and bake 20 to 25 minutes, until top is golden brown. Keeps five days at room temperature.

INSIDER TIPS
- Quick fix
- Substitute butterscotch or peanut butter chips for the chocolate and call them Butterscotch Chip Bars or Peanut Butter Chip Bars.

CATEGORIES
- Nut free

Cranberry Apple Bars

A hearty fruit bar to welcome the apple season.

Yield: 1 8x8-inch pan

Crust and topping

- 1 cup flour
- 1 cup oats, regular or quick
- ¾ cup sugar
- ¼ teaspoon salt
- ¼ pound (1 stick) melted butter

Filling

- 3 large sliced apples (approximately 3 cups), peeled or unpeeled
- 1 cup chopped fresh cranberries or ½ cup dried cranberries
- ½ cup sugar
- ¼ cup flour
- 1 tablespoon lemon juice
- 1 teaspoon cinnamon
- ¼ teaspoon nutmeg
- ¼ teaspoon allspice

1. Preheat oven to 350° F. and lightly grease pan.

2. For crust, mix flour, oats, sugar, and salt in a medium bowl. Add melted butter and mix until crumbly.

3. Press half of crumbs into pan and bake 20 minutes. Cool for a few minutes.

4. While crust is baking, mix apples, cranberries, sugar, flour, lemon juice, cinnamon, nutmeg, and allspice in a large bowl. Carefully spread filling over crust. Don't worry if it seems too lumpy in some areas. Just gently press down fruit. Top with remaining crumbs.

5. Bake 45 to 60 minutes, until apple filling bubbles up around sides of pan and oats begin to turn light brown. Keeps at room temperature for two days. Refrigerate if keeping longer.

INSIDER TIPS

- Instead of dried cranberries, use raisins.
- Leave out cranberries and drizzle with caramel after baking.
- Use a mixture of apples and pears.
- Substitute any fresh or canned fruit, such as pears, plums, or peaches.

CATEGORIES

- Whole grain
- Nut free
- Egg free

Date Bars

These traditional bars are one hundred percent whole grain, but don't taste "healthy" or cause suspicion with customers looking for a tasty treat.

Yield: 1 8x8-inch pan

Filling

- 1 ½ cups (8-ounce tub) pitted dates
- 2 cups water

Crust and topping

- 1 cup rolled oats, regular or quick
- 1 cup whole wheat pastry flour
- ½ cup brown sugar
- 1 teaspoon cinnamon
- ¼ teaspoon salt
- ¼ pound (1 stick) butter

1. Soak dates in hot water for at least one hour. Drain excess water and mash or squeeze dates through your fingers until no large pieces remain. Remove any pits. (This is a good job for kids or unwanted visitors. It's not hard, just messy, and they won't want to bother you again.)

2. Preheat oven to 350° F. and lightly grease pan.

3. Mix together oats, flour, sugar, cinnamon, and salt in a medium bowl. Blend in the butter (using a mixer or by hand) until large crumbs form.

4. Press two-thirds of dough onto the pan bottom, patting down hard to form the crust. Spread date filling over crust and sprinkle with remaining mixture.

5. Bake 30 to 35 minutes, until the top crust is a medium golden brown. Keeps one week at room temperature or two weeks refrigerated.

INSIDER TIPS

- Crust recipe can be used as streusel for any product.
- Soak dates in orange or apple juice.
- Use other dried fruits such as apricots, figs, or raisins.

CATEGORIES

- Whole grain
- Egg free
- Nut free

Honey Oat Bars

These soft chewy bars with no added fat are a great morning treat.

Yield: 1 8x8-inch pan

- 1 cup honey
- 2 cups rolled oats
- 1 teaspoon cinnamon
- $^1/_8$ teaspoon salt
- 1 cup raisins
- ½ cup dried cranberries
- ½ cup chopped apricots

1. Preheat oven to 350° F. and lightly grease pan.

2. Heat honey in a medium saucepan, then stir in oats, cinnamon, salt, and dried fruits.

3. Press mixture into prepared pan and bake 30 to 35 minutes, until light brown around edges.

4. Cut bars while still warm. Keeps two weeks.

INSIDER TIPS
- Quick fix
- Crumble and bag for sale as Honey Oat Clusters.

CATEGORIES
- Whole grain
- Dairy free
- Egg free
- Nut free

Lemon Blueberry Cream Bars

Sweet and tart, this recipe works with any seasonal berry.

Yield: 1 9x13-inch pan

Crust and topping

- 2 cups flour
- 1 ½ cups quick oats
- 1 cup sugar
- ½ teaspoon salt
- ½ teaspoon baking soda
- 6 ounces (1½ sticks) butter

Filling

- 1 large egg
- 1 (14-ounce) can sweetened condensed milk
- ½ cup lemon juice
- 3 cups blueberries

1. Preheat oven to 350° F. and grease pan.
2. Combine flour, oats, sugar, salt, and baking soda in a large bowl. Add butter and mix until crumbs form.
3. Reserve 1 cup crumbs for topping and press remaining crumbs onto bottom of prepared pan. Bake 15 to 20 minutes, until a light golden brown.
4. While crust is baking, beat together egg, condensed milk, and lemon juice in a medium bowl.
5. Let crust cool for several minutes, then sprinkle on blueberries and evenly pour filling on top. Space the berries and spread filling to cover dough.
6. Sprinkle on remaining crumbs and bake 25 to 30 minutes until streusel is light brown.
7. Chill before cutting. Bars keep several days in fridge.

INSIDER TIPS

- Lemon Raspberry is a nice follow-up to blueberry season.
- Bake mixed berry bars using any combination of three or more berries.
- Before adding crumb topping sprinkle with 1 cup (6-ounce) bag white chocolate chips.

CATEGORIES

- Nut free

Oatmeal Breakfast Bars

Customers love bar cookies for breakfast and these are much healthier than donuts.

Yield: 1 8x8-inch pan

- ¼ cup oil
- ½ cup brown sugar
- 1 large egg
- 1 teaspoon vanilla
- 1 cup whole wheat pastry flour
- 1 cup rolled oats
- 1 teaspoon cinnamon
- ½ teaspoon baking soda
- ¼ teaspoon salt
- ½ cup raisins

1. Preheat oven to 350° F. and grease pan.

2. Mix together oil, sugar, egg, and vanilla in a large bowl. Stir in flour, oats, cinnamon, baking soda, and salt. Add raisins and stir.

3. Press into prepared pan. Bake 25 to 35 minutes until a light golden brown. Keeps up to five days at room temperature.

INSIDER TIPS
- Quick fix
- Substitute any dried fruit for raisins.
- Add 1 cup granola.

CATEGORIES
- Whole grain
- Dairy free
- Nut free

Peanut Butter Granola Bars

This is the easiest no-bake bar recipe. Use any granola you have on hand.

Yield: 1 8x8-inch pan

- 1 cup honey
- ½ cup peanut butter
- 3 cups granola, crumbled into small pieces

1. Grease pan.

2. In medium saucepan, boil honey and peanut butter for 1 minute over medium heat, then stir in granola.

3. Press evenly into prepared pan. Cut while warm. Leave in pan to cool. Keeps for several weeks.

INSIDER TIPS
- Quick fix
- If you're selling at a farmers' market, use local honey and let customers know it's local.
- Add ½ cup raisins.

CATEGORIES
- Whole grain
- Dairy free
- Egg free

Pecan Chocolate Chip Pie Bars

These bars, a chocolate version of pecan pie, sell well all year.

Yield: 1 8x8-inch pan

Crust

- ¼ pound (1 stick) butter
- ¼ cup granulated sugar
- 1 ¼ cups flour

Filling

- 2 large eggs
- ¾ cup light or dark corn syrup
- ¾ cup brown sugar
- 1 tablespoon butter, melted
- 1 teaspoon vanilla
- ⅛ teaspoon rum extract
- ⅛ teaspoon salt
- 1 cup chopped pecans
- 1 cup (6-ounce bag) chocolate chips

1. Preheat oven to 350° F. and grease pan bottom and ½ inch up sides.

2. Cream butter, sugar, and flour in a medium bowl. Press into bottom of pan and bake 20 to 25 minutes until light golden brown.

3. While crust is baking, mix together eggs, corn syrup, sugar, butter, extracts, and salt in a medium bowl. Stir in pecans and chocolate chips. Spread over warm crust. Push nuts and chips to evenly cover. Bake another 30 to 40 minutes, until filling is a light golden brown around edges and top feels firm when gently pressed.

4. While still warm, run a knife around the perimeter to loosen filling from pan. Cool, then chill before cutting. Keeps one week at room temperature.

INSIDER TIPS

- Substitute walnuts for pecans.
- Substitute honey for corn syrup.
- For Pecan Pie Bars, omit chocolate chips.

Raspberry Peach Custard Bars

This attractive bar has a thick custard-like filling studded with chopped peach and berries.

Yield: 1 8x8-inch pan

Crust and topping

- 1 ½ cups flour
- ¾ cup sugar
- ⅛ teaspoon salt
- 6 ounces (1 ½ sticks) cold butter

Filling

- 2 large eggs
- 1 cup sugar
- ½ cup sour cream
- 1 teaspoon vanilla
- ½ cup flour
- ⅛ teaspoon salt
- 2 cups raspberries
- 1 large peach, chopped (approximately 1 cup)

1. Preheat oven to 350° F. and grease pan.

2. For crust and topping, combine flour, sugar, and salt in a medium bowl. Cut in the butter until pieces are small and evenly distributed.

3. Reserve 1 cup for topping and press remaining crumbs evenly into prepared pan. Bake 20 to 25 minutes, until crust is a light golden brown.

4. While crust is baking, beat together eggs, sugar, sour cream, vanilla, flour, and salt in a large bowl. Stir in fruit.

5. Let crust cool for several minutes, then pour fruit custard over crust. Distribute berries and peaches so they are in one layer. Sprinkle topping over filling and bake for 45 to 55 minutes, until topping is light brown.

6. Cool to room temperature, then refrigerate. Cut when cold. Keeps several days in fridge.

INSIDER TIPS

- Substitute full-fat plain yogurt for sour cream.
- Can be made with any seasonal fruit, such as blueberries and nectarines.

CATEGORIES

- Nut free

Southern Fruit Bars

This crust recipe began as a mistake. My assistant had forgotten to add Amaretto when making batter for two dozen Amaretto cakes. She offered to throw it out and start again, but I told her to refrigerate the dense dough. Surely I could do something with it.

Yield: 1 10x15-inch jelly roll pan

- ¼ pound (1 stick) butter
- 1 cup sugar
- 1 large egg
- ½ teaspoon vanilla
- 2 cups flour
- 1 ½ teaspoons baking powder
- ¼ teaspoon salt
- 1 ½ cups jam, any flavor (strawberry or apricot are customer favorites)
- 1 cup sliced almonds

1. Cream butter and sugar in a large bowl. Add egg and vanilla, mixing thoroughly.

2. Add flour, baking powder, and salt; mix until there are no streaks of flour. At this point you can use immediately or wrap the dough and refrigerate for up to two weeks.

3. Preheat oven to 350° F. and grease pan.

4. Roll out dough on a heavily floured surface and transfer to prepared pan. Press to fit bottom and slightly up the sides. Push together any torn dough or thin spots. Spread with jam and sprinkle with almonds.

5. Bake 20 to 30 minutes, until crust edges and almonds are medium golden brown. Keeps two weeks.

INSIDER TIPS
- Instead of almonds, use any streusel (Chapter 15).
- If cutting and stacking bars for storage, use waxed paper or plastic wrap between layers.
- To bake as a tart, use different colored jams (such as raspberry and apricot) and swirl together.
- Why are these called Southern? I dunno, it sounded good at the time.

Chapter 10

Muffins

Muffins have been traditional breakfast and mid-morning fare, but now they've become popular for snacking at any time of the day. So whether your customers like muffins that are overly sweet to barely sweet, made with whole grains or white flour, with fresh produce or simply plain, you'll find a muffin recipe in this chapter to suit your target market.

We made so many different muffin varieties that we displayed ten basic flavors daily, and then rotated others throughout the month, depending upon fresh produce, customer requests, and our creative instincts. I always had a variety to suit both the health food folks and those who wanted something more cake-like.

To differentiate between true muffins and cake muffins, look at the recipe ingredients. Those with a low amount of fat and sweetener (¼ cup or less of each, per one dozen medium-sized muffins) are true muffins. Those with a high amount of fat and sweetener (½ cup or more of each per one dozen batch) are really un-iced cupcakes. Cake for breakfast!

Low fat muffins have a fairly short shelf life and generally last no more than two days. Cake-like muffins with higher fat can keep several days. So the less fat, the shorter the shelf life. The more fat, the tastier your customers will find them. As you read through the recipes you'll see which ones are really cakes.

Tips for Baking:
- Muffins bake best in a hot oven, 375-400° F. Larger muffins may need a temperature reduction if the tops get too dark but the centers are not baked.

- If your muffins typically get a split on top with batter oozing through, then your oven runs a little hot. Always reduce the temperature by 25° F.

- All batters can be mixed and refrigerated for several days. Stir before using. Butter-based batters will be thick but can still be used directly from the fridge. For cold batters, add an extra minute or two for baking time.

- Use an ice-cream scoop for portion control.

- All muffin batters can be baked as loaves or coffeecakes.

- Conversely, most of the recipes listed in the coffeecakes or sweetbreads chapters may be baked as muffins.

- Before baking, add a streusel topping or sprinkle of sugar.

Tips for Handling:
- I like paper liners because paper keeps muffins moister and there's less to clean up.

- Directly after baking, leave muffins in their pans for at least a few minutes or they may lose shape. Finish cooling in the pan or on a rack.

Variations:
- Experiment using different produce for any of the recipes.
- Sizing
  - Large muffins have a 2 ¼-inch bottom, 1 ¾-inch wall
  - Medium muffins have a 2-inch bottom, 1 ¼-inch wall

- All recipes for 12 medium muffins will make 6 large muffins.

- If you want muffins with a large head, use more batter to make them bigger. Forget the "two-thirds full" rule and fill to the top. But make sure the batter is thick or it will flow over the pan sides before the top sets.

- Mini muffins are nice for catering or sold by the dozen. The small size is best not sold individually or you'll be making twenty-five cent sales all day.

- After baking, add glaze or string icing.

Chocolate Coconut Muffins

Apple Oat Muffins

I developed this hearty recipe after many requests for whole grain oat muffins.

Yield: 12 medium muffins

- ¼ cup oil
- ¼ cup sugar
- 1 large egg
- ¾ cup apple juice
- 1 cup whole wheat pastry flour
- 1 cup regular or quick oats
- 1 tablespoon baking powder
- ⅛ teaspoon baking soda
- 2 teaspoons cinnamon
- ½ teaspoon nutmeg
- ½ teaspoon salt
- 1 medium apple, finely chopped, with skin
- 1 cup raisins

1. Preheat oven to 375° F. and place paper cups in muffin pan.

2. Beat together oil, sugar, egg, and juice in a medium bowl.

3. In a separate bowl, stir together flour, oats, baking powder, baking soda, cinnamon, nutmeg, and salt. Pour dry ingredients into wet and stir gently until mixed. Some small lumps are okay. Stir in apples and raisins. The batter will be very thick.

4. Divide evenly into muffin cups, filling pans almost to top. Bake 20 to 25 minutes, until a finger pressed gently on top leaves no imprint. Keeps fresh two days at room temperature.

INSIDER TIPS
- Substitute 1 medium finely chopped pear.
- Before baking, top with an oat streusel or raw sugar.

CATEGORIES
- Whole grain
- Dairy free
- Nut free

Banana Corn Muffins

An unusual and tasty combination, another winning recipe from my baker, Saraly.

Yield: 12 medium muffins

- 1 cup (2 small) bananas, mashed
- $^1/_3$ cup oil
- ¼ cup sugar
- 1 large egg
- ½ cup milk
- 1 ¼ cups flour
- $^2/_3$ cup yellow cornmeal
- 1 tablespoon baking powder
- ½ teaspoon salt

1. Preheat oven to 375° F. and place paper cups in muffin pan.

2. Combine bananas, oil, sugar, egg, and milk in a large bowl.

3. Stir in flour, cornmeal, baking powder, and salt.

4. Divide evenly into muffin cups, filling pans almost to top. Bake 20 to 25 minutes, until a finger pressed gently on top leaves no imprint, or a toothpick inserted into a muffin center comes out dry. Keeps two days at room temperature.

INSIDER TIPS
- Quick fix
- Add ½ cup corn kernels.
- Substitute 1 cup whole wheat pastry flour for all-purpose.

CATEGORIES
- Nut free

Banana Walnut Muffins

This is a classic must-have item for every baker's product line.

Yield: 12 medium muffins

- 2 cups (3 medium or 4 small) bananas, mashed
- ¼ cup oil
- ½ cup sugar
- 1 large egg
- 1 cup buttermilk
- 2 teaspoons vanilla
- 1 ¼ cups whole wheat pastry flour
- 1 ¼ cups all-purpose flour
- 1 ½ teaspoons baking soda
- 1 teaspoon baking powder
- ½ teaspoon salt
- ½ cup chopped walnuts

1. Preheat oven to 375° F. and place paper cups in muffin pan.

2. Beat together bananas, oil, sugar, egg, buttermilk, and vanilla in a large bowl.

3. In a medium bowl, stir together the flours, baking soda, baking powder, and salt. Pour dry ingredients into wet and stir gently until mixed. Some small lumps are okay. Stir in walnuts. Batter will be very thick.

4. Divide evenly into muffin cups, filling pans almost to top. Bake 18 to 22 minutes. Muffins are done when a finger pressed gently on top leaves no imprint. Keeps two or three days.

INSIDER TIPS
- Before baking, top with streusel or chopped walnuts.
- Add I cup blueberries and ¼ cup additional whole wheat pastry flour.

CATEGORIES
- Whole grain

Berry Almond Muffins

These were my best selling muffins, gorgeous and delicious. We used this recipe for two varieties, Blueberry Muffins with a sprinkling of granulated sugar before baking, and Raspberry Almond Muffins topped with a few sliced almonds.

Yield: 12 medium muffins

- ¼ pound (1 stick) butter
- ¾ cup sugar
- 1 large egg
- 2 ¾ cups flour
- 1 tablespoon baking powder
- ¼ teaspoon baking soda
- ¼ teaspoon salt
- ¾ cup buttermilk
- 6 tablespoons Amaretto (or use water, or more buttermilk)
- 1 ½ teaspoons almond extract
- 4 ounces fresh or frozen berries (not in syrup), approximately 1 cup
- sliced almonds for garnish, optional

1. Preheat oven to 375° F. and place paper cups in muffin pan.

2. Cream butter and sugar in a large mixer bowl. Add egg and continue to mix.

3. In a separate bowl, mix together flour, baking powder, baking soda, and salt.

4. Pour Amaretto, buttermilk, and almond extract into a large measuring cup.

5. Alternately add the wet and dry ingredients to the mixer bowl, beginning and ending with the dry ingredients. Scrape down the bowl several times to be sure all the batter is thoroughly mixed in. The thick batter should drop easily from a spoon. If it seems too stiff, add a little more buttermilk.

6. Scoop batter evenly into muffin cups and fill almost to the top. Evenly space 5 or 6 berries on top of each muffin. Gently press most of the berries at least halfway down into the batter. It's okay to leave 1 or 2 partially exposed. Sprinkle almonds on top, if using.

7. Bake 25 to 30 minutes, or until lightly browned. The muffins should feel firm when gently pressed on top. If they are getting too dark but are still slightly wet inside, turn heat down to 350° F. Keeps three or four days.

INSIDER TIPS

- Don't mix berries into batter. Doing so may cause unsightly streaks of color, plus adding them on top will ensure each muffin has same number of berries.
- Use any fresh berry. Frozen berries are fine for off-season, but keep frozen until ready to use.
- Before baking, top with streusel (Chapter 15).
- Glaze after baking.
- Make into cupcakes by frosting with buttercream (Chapter 15).

Buttermilk Honey Muffins

I created this recipe as a cupcake, but it begged to be a muffin. It's light, tender, and luscious, perfect for incorporating seasonal fruit.

Yield: 12 medium muffins

- ¼ pound (1 stick) butter, melted
- ½ cup honey
- ½ cup brown sugar
- ¾ cup buttermilk
- 2 large eggs
- 1 teaspoon vanilla
- 2 ¾ cups flour
- 2 teaspoons baking powder
- 1 teaspoon baking soda
- ½ teaspoon salt

1. Preheat oven to 375° F. and place paper cups in muffin pan.

2. Combine butter, honey, brown sugar, buttermilk, eggs, and vanilla in a medium bowl.

3. Add flour, baking powder, baking soda, and salt. Mix until no lumps are visible.

4. Divide evenly into muffin cups, filling pans almost to top. Bake 18 to 25 minutes, until a finger pressed lightly on a muffin top leaves no imprint. Stays soft and moist for several days.

INSIDER TIPS
- Quick fix
- Add 1 cup diced fresh fruit and ¼ cup additional flour.
- Before baking, top with streusel (Chapter 15).
- Delicious with honey butter.

CATEGORIES
- Nut free

Carrot Muffins

A customer told me about adding ricotta cheese to muffins for added moisture. These are protein packed and tender.

Yield: 12 medium muffins

- ¼ cup oil
- ½ cup sugar
- 2 large eggs
- 1 cup ricotta cheese
- 1 cup buttermilk
- 2 teaspoons vanilla
- 1 ¼ cups whole wheat pastry flour
- 1 ¼ cups all-purpose flour
- 2 teaspoons baking soda
- 1 teaspoon baking powder
- 2 teaspoons cinnamon
- ½ teaspoon salt
- 2 cups grated carrots

1. Preheat oven to 375° F. and place paper cups in muffin pan.

2. In a medium bowl, beat together oil, sugar, eggs, ricotta, buttermilk, and vanilla.

3. In a separate bowl stir together flours, baking soda, baking powder, cinnamon, and salt. Pour dry ingredients into wet and stir gently until mixed. Some small lumps are okay. Mix in carrots. Batter will be very thick.

4. Divide evenly into muffin cups, filling pans almost to top. Bake 18 to 25 minutes, until a finger pressed gently on top leaves no imprint. Keeps two days at room temperature or one week in fridge.

INSIDER TIPS
- The addition of ricotta works for most muffin recipes.
- Add ½ cup raisins or chopped dried dates.
- Add ¼ teaspoon each nutmeg and ginger.
- Before baking, top with raw sugar.

CATEGORIES
- Whole grain
- Nut free

Chocolate Coconut Muffins

These are extra moist with a deep, rich chocolate flavor.

Yield: 12 medium muffins

- $^1/_3$ cup oil
- $^1/_3$ cup sugar
- 1 large egg
- 2 teaspoons vanilla
- ½ cup cottage cheese
- 1 cup buttermilk
- 2 cups flour
- ½ cup cocoa
- 2 teaspoons baking powder
- ½ teaspoon baking soda
- ½ teaspoon salt
- ½ cup coconut, plus ¼ cup additional for topping

1. Preheat oven to 375° F. and place paper cups in muffin pan.

2. In a medium bowl, beat together oil, sugar, egg, vanilla, cottage cheese, and buttermilk.

3. In a separate bowl, stir together flour, cocoa, baking powder, baking soda, and salt. Pour dry ingredients into wet and mix to a thick batter. Some small lumps are okay. Stir in ½ cup coconut.

4. Divide evenly into muffin cups, filling pans almost to top. Sprinkle on extra coconut. Bake 20 to 25 minutes until a finger pressed gently on top leaves no imprint. Turn down heat 25° F. if the tops are getting too brown. Keeps two days at room temperature, one week in fridge.

INSIDER TIPS
- For Chocolate Raspberry, substitute 1 cup raspberries instead of coconut.
- For Double Chocolate Coconut, stir in 1 cup chocolate chips.

CATEGORIES
- Nut free

Chunky Pear Muffins

This moist and spicy low-fat seasonal muffin sells well throughout the fall.

Yield: 12 medium muffins

- 2 medium pears grated, with skin
- 2 tablespoons oil
- ¼ cup sugar
- 1 large egg
- ½ cup apple juice or water
- 1 teaspoon vanilla
- 1 cup whole wheat pastry flour
- 1 cup all-purpose flour
- 1 teaspoon baking powder
- 1 teaspoon baking soda
- ½ teaspoon salt
- 1 teaspoon cinnamon
- ½ teaspoon nutmeg
- 1 medium pear, chopped, with skin

1. Preheat oven to 375° F. and place paper cups in muffin pan.

2. Grate pears and put into a medium bowl with the oil, sugar, egg, juice, and vanilla. Mix well.

3. In a separate bowl stir together both flours, baking powder, baking soda, salt, cinnamon, and nutmeg. Pour dry ingredients into wet and stir gently until mixed. Some small lumps are okay. Stir in chopped pear.

4. Divide evenly into muffin pans, filling pans almost to the top. Bake 20 to 25 minutes. Muffins are done when a finger pressed gently on top leaves no imprint. Keeps two days at room temperature.

INSIDER TIPS
- Peeling only wastes time. After baking, the skin is not noticeable.
- Apples are an excellent substitute for pears.
- Before baking, top with streusel (Chapter 15) or raw sugar.

CATEGORIES
- Whole grain
- Dairy free
- Nut free

Coconut Cranberry Muffins

I created these lower-fat muffins to expand our holiday season product line.

Yield: 12 medium muffins

- $^1/_3$ cup oil
- $^1/_3$ cup sugar
- 1 large egg
- 1 teaspoon vanilla
- 1 cup buttermilk
- 2 ½ cups flour
- 2 teaspoons baking powder
- ½ teaspoon baking soda
- ½ teaspoon salt
- ½ cup chopped cranberries, fresh or dried
- ½ cup coconut, plus ¼ cup additional for topping

1. Preheat oven to 375° F. and place paper cups in muffin pan.

2. In a medium bowl, beat together oil, sugar, egg, vanilla, and buttermilk.

3. In a separate bowl, stir together flour, baking powder, baking soda, and salt. Pour dry ingredients into wet and mix to a thick batter. Some small lumps are okay. Stir in cranberries and coconut.

4. Divide evenly into muffin cups, filling pans almost to top. Sprinkle extra coconut on top. Bake 20 to 25 minutes until a finger pressed gently on top leaves no imprint. Turn down heat if the tops are getting too brown. Keeps two days.

INSIDER TIPS
- Quick fix
- For Coconut Orange Cranberry Muffins, use orange extract instead of vanilla and substitute orange juice for buttermilk.
- For the week before Christmas, instead of coconut on top add a green buttercream (Chapter 15) holly leaf decoration with 3 little cranberry pieces for the berries. Customers love the special touch.

CATEGORIES
- Nut free

Corn and Cheese Muffins

These sell well throughout the day. Add bits of red and green peppers for an eye-catching display.

Yield: 12 medium muffins

- 2 large eggs
- ¼ cup oil
- 1 ½ cups buttermilk
- 2 cups flour
- 1 cup yellow cornmeal
- 2 tablespoons sugar
- 1 ½ teaspoons baking soda
- 1 teaspoon salt
- 1 cup shredded cheddar cheese

1. Preheat oven to 375° F. and place paper cups in muffin pan.

2. In a medium bowl, beat together eggs, oil, and buttermilk.

3. In a separate bowl combine flour, cornmeal, sugar, baking soda, and salt. Add cheese and mix thoroughly. Stir dry ingredients into the wet. Batter should be very thick. If too thin, add flour. If too thick, add more buttermilk.

4. Divide evenly into muffin cups, filling pans almost to the top. Bake 15 to 20 minutes until tops feel dry and firm when gently pressed. Turn heat down if edges look too dark. Keeps two days at room temperature, or several if refrigerated.

INSIDER TIPS
- Quick fix
- Add ½ cup finely chopped onions.
- Add ¼ cup each, finely diced red and green pepper.
- Use any sharp cheese instead of cheddar.

CATEGORIES
- Nut free

Country Health Muffins

We made this muffin using baker Saraly's pumpkin bread recipe and they sold well from Thanksgiving to Christmas. Customers loved the spicy flavor and moist texture, but sales always dropped off after the holidays. When I tweaked the spices and changed the name to Country Health Muffins, sales became steady year round.

Yield: 18-24 medium muffins

- 2 ½ cups sugar
- ¾ cup oil
- 3 large eggs
- 1½ cups (15-ounce can) pumpkin puree
- ½ cup water, apple cider, or orange juice
- 1 ½ cups whole wheat pastry flour
- 1 ½ cups all-purpose flour
- 2 teaspoons baking soda
- 1 teaspoon salt
- 2 teaspoons cinnamon
- 1 teaspoon ginger
- ½ teaspoon allspice

1. Preheat oven to 375° F. and place paper cups in muffin pans.
2. In a large bowl, mix together sugar, oil, eggs, pumpkin, and water.
3. In a separate bowl, stir together flours, baking soda, salt, cinnamon, ginger, and allspice. Pour dry ingredients into wet. Batter will be thin.
4. Divide evenly into muffin cups, filling pans almost to top. Bake 20 to 25 minutes until the tops appear dry and a finger pressed gently on top leaves no imprint. Keeps several days at room temperature.

INSIDER TIPS
- For seasonal addition, use I cup chopped apple or pear.
- Add 1 cup raisins.
- This recipe makes excellent pumpkin bread.

CATEGORIES
- Whole grain
- Dairy free
- Nut free

Glorious Morning Muffins

Whole grain "cupcakes" for breakfast.

Yield: 12 medium muffins

- ½ cup oil
- ½ cup brown sugar
- 2 large eggs
- ½ cup orange or apple juice
- 2 teaspoons vanilla
- 2 cups whole wheat pastry flour
- 2 teaspoons baking soda
- 2 teaspoons cinnamon
- ½ teaspoon salt
- 2 cups grated zucchini
- 1 large apple, chopped, with skin
- ½ cup coconut
- ½ cup chopped pecans
- ½ cup raisins

1. Preheat oven to 375° F. and place paper cups in muffin pan.

2. In a medium bowl, beat together oil, sugar, eggs, juice, and vanilla.

3. In a separate bowl, stir together flour, baking soda, cinnamon, and salt. Pour dry ingredients into wet, and stir gently until mixed. Some small lumps are okay.

4. Mix in the zucchini, apple, coconut, pecans, and raisins. Batter will be very thick.

5. Divide evenly into muffin cups, filling pans almost to top. Bake 20 to 25 minutes until a finger pressed gently on top leaves no imprint. Keeps several days at room temperature.

INSIDER TIPS
- Make Glorious Carrot Muffins by using grated carrots instead of zucchini.
- Add ½ cup crushed pineapple, drained.
- Turn these into cupcakes by adding cream cheese icing (Chapter 15).

CATEGORIES
- Whole grain
- Dairy free

Honey Yogurt Muffins

Whole grain and low in fat.

Yield: 12 medium muffins

- ¼ cup oil
- ¼ cup honey
- 1 large egg
- 1 cup fat-free yogurt, plain or vanilla
- ¼ cup lemon juice
- 1 cup whole wheat pastry flour
- 1 cup all-purpose flour
- 1 ½ teaspoons baking soda
- ½ teaspoon salt
- ½ teaspoon nutmeg

1. Preheat oven to 375° F. and place paper cups in muffin pan.

2. In a medium bowl, beat together oil, honey, egg, yogurt, and lemon juice.

3. In a separate bowl, stir together the whole wheat flour, all-purpose flour, baking soda, salt, and nutmeg. Pour dry ingredients into wet and stir until mixed. Some small lumps are okay.

4. Divide evenly into muffin cups, filling pans almost to top. Bake 18 to 25 minutes until a finger pressed gently on top leaves no imprint. Keeps two days.

INSIDER TIPS
- Quick fix
- Add 1 cup fresh chopped seasonal fruit (peaches or blueberries are nice) and add additional ¼ cup flour.
- Add 1 cup dried cranberries or raisins.
- Before baking, top with streusel (Chapter 15).

CATEGORIES
- Whole grain
- Nut free

Maple Walnut Muffins

A customer said he would only eat muffins if they tasted as good as pancakes. The challenge was on! These muffins have a lovely golden glow and taste like pancakes with syrup.

Yield: 12 medium muffins

- ¼ pound (1 stick) butter
- ¾ cup brown sugar
- 1 large egg
- 2 teaspoons maple extract
- 2 ¾ cups all purpose flour
- 1 ½ teaspoons baking powder
- 1 teaspoon baking soda
- ¼ teaspoon salt
- 1 cup milk
- 1 ½ cups large walnut pieces

1. Preheat oven to 375° F. and place paper cups in muffin pan.

2. Cream butter and sugar in a medium bowl. Beat in egg and maple extract.

3. In a separate bowl, combine flour, baking powder, baking soda, and salt.

4. Alternately add the dry ingredients and the milk, to the butter mixture, beginning and ending with the dry. Scrape bowl several times to make sure batter is mixed.

5. Divide evenly into muffin cups, filling pans almost to top. Place walnut halves on top, squeezing in as many as possible to cover the entire surface. Press nuts lightly into batter. Bake 20 to 25 minutes or until muffins are light golden brown and firm when top is gently pressed. Keeps several days at room temperature.

INSIDER TIPS
- Add ½ cup chopped walnuts to batter.
- To make mini-muffins, center one large walnut half on top of each muffin.
- For Maple Cream Cupcakes, chop walnuts and add to the batter. Frost with vanilla or maple buttercream (Chapter 15). Sprinkle more chopped nuts on top.

Nectarine Blueberry Muffins

Every year when the blueberry and nectarine seasons overlapped, these muffins sold out first.

Yield: 12 medium muffins

- $^1/_3$ cup oil
- $^1/_3$ cup sugar
- 1 large egg
- 1 ¼ cups buttermilk
- 1 teaspoon vanilla
- 1 ¼ cups whole wheat pastry flour
- 1 ¼ cups all-purpose flour
- 1 tablespoon baking powder
- ½ teaspoon baking soda
- ½ teaspoon nutmeg
- ½ teaspoon salt
- 2 medium nectarines, chopped
- ½ cup blueberries

1. Preheat oven to 375° F. and place paper cups in muffin pan.

2. In a medium bowl, beat together oil, sugar, egg, buttermilk, and vanilla.

3. In a separate bowl, stir together both flours, baking powder, baking soda, nutmeg, and salt. Pour dry ingredients into wet and stir until mixed. The batter will be very thick. Some small lumps are okay. Stir in fruit.

4. Divide evenly into muffin cups, filling pans almost to top and mounding any excess batter. Bake 20 to 25 minutes or until a light golden brown and a finger pressed gently on top leaves no imprint. Keeps two days.

INSIDER TIPS
- Use any seasonal fruit, such as peaches or plums.
- Add ½ cup coconut.
- Top with raw sugar before baking.

CATEGORIES
- Whole grain
- Nut free

Pineapple Muffins

Moist and soft with a tender bite, these also make a flavorful pineapple blueberry muffin. I developed this recipe because I love pineapple. So did my customers when I added these to our menu.

Yield: 12 medium muffins

- $^1/_3$ cup oil
- ½ cup brown sugar
- 1 large egg
- 1 cup sour cream
- 1 (8-ounce) can crushed pineapple, with juice
- 1 teaspoon vanilla
- 2 ½ cups flour
- 2 teaspoons baking powder
- ½ teaspoon baking soda
- ½ teaspoon salt

1. Preheat oven to 375° F. and place paper cups in muffin pan.

2. In medium bowl combine oil, brown sugar, egg, sour cream, pineapple, and vanilla.

3. Add flour, baking powder, baking soda and salt, and mix until no flour lumps are visible.

4. Divide evenly into muffin cups, filling pans almost to top. Bake 18 to 20 minutes, until a finger pressed lightly on top leaves no imprint. These stay soft and moist for several days.

INSIDER TIPS
- Quick fix
- Add 1 cup blueberries for Pineapple Blueberry Muffins.
- Add ¼ teaspoon nutmeg.
- After baking, glaze or add string icing (Chapter 15).

CATEGORIES
- Nut free

Plum Good Muffins

A quick fix to start off any work day.

Yield: 12 medium muffins

- ¼ cup oil
- ¼ cup sugar
- 1 large egg
- 1 cup milk
- 2 ½ cups whole wheat pastry flour
- 1 tablespoon baking powder
- ½ teaspoon salt
- 3 medium plums, chopped

1. Preheat oven to 375° F. and place paper cups in muffin pan.

2. Beat together the oil, sugar, egg, and milk in a medium bowl.

3. Add flour, baking powder and salt then stir until mixed. Some small lumps are okay. Stir in plums. The batter will be very thick.

4. Divide evenly into muffin cups, filling pans almost to top. Bake 20 to 25 minutes, until a finger pressed gently on top leaves no imprint. Keeps two days.

INSIDER TIPS
- Quick fix
- Use any seasonal fruits, such as nectarines or pears.
- Add 1 teaspoon cinnamon and ½ teaspoon ground ginger.
- Before baking top with raw sugar.

CATEGORIES
- Whole grain
- Nut free

Savory Cheese 'n Veggie Muffins

I enjoy a challenge, so when I read that all baked goods must have sugar because it's "critical in the creaming process," I developed several recipes without any sweetener. These muffins, a meal in themselves, have a light, soft texture.

Yield: 12 medium muffins

- 2 ½ cups flour
- 1 tablespoon baking powder
- ½ teaspoon salt
- ½ teaspoon coarse ground black pepper
- 1 cup shredded cheese, any variety
- 1 cup (cooked or fresh) chopped vegetables, such as peppers or zucchini
- 2 large eggs
- ¼ cup oil
- 1 cup milk

1. Preheat oven to 375° F. and place paper cups in muffin pan.

2. Combine flour, baking powder, salt, and pepper in a medium bowl. Stir in cheese and vegetables.

3. In another bowl, beat together eggs, oil, and milk.

4. Pour liquid into the dry and mix well. Batter should be thick and plop when scooped out. If too thin, add flour. If too thick add more milk.

5. Divide evenly into muffin cups, filling pans almost to top. Bake 20 to 25 minutes, until a finger pressed gently on top leaves no imprint. Turn heat down if edges look too dark. Keeps several days in fridge.

6. Store cold but can be left at room temperature up to 2 hours while selling.

INSIDER TIPS
- Quick fix
- Label as made with no sugar – customers will love it.
- Add 2 tablespoons chopped fresh herbs, such as rosemary, dill, or thyme.

CATEGORIES
- Nut free

Chapter 11

Pound Cakes and Bundt Cakes

I selected the recipes in this chapter for their diverse flavors, appeal, and popularity. Pound cakes have a fine crumb with a firm, moist, tender grain and a rich buttery taste. Bundt cakes have a cake-like taste and texture. Bundt refers to the shape – a ring or tube shape with a decorative bottom. When the cake is finished baking, it's turned upside down so the bottom becomes an attractive top. They're easy to decorate with a sifting of confectioners' sugar, which highlights the pan design and makes an eye-catching cake.

Pound cakes and bundt cakes are usually perceived as fancier than coffeecakes, so they're often found at celebrations and special events, whether these events are small informal family gatherings or larger affairs.

For larger celebrations, customers will buy a full-sized bundt cake or pound cake, which has up to 24 servings. But for informal gatherings or small social events, smaller cakes sell far better than the larger cakes. For retail sales at farmers' markets, bring smaller cakes for sale and take orders for the larger cakes. I suggest having both pan sizes to meet all customer needs.

Individual slices also sell well packaged with a plastic fork. Find the recipes you like and experiment with selling both slices and whole small bundt cakes. Sales results will tell you which works best for your customer base.

Tips for Baking:
- Batters can be refrigerated for several days before baking. Stir before pouring into pan.

- Cakes are done when they pull away from the sides of the pan, have a medium dark golden color, and pass the toothpick test (in accordance with the federal no-cake-left-behind rule).

- The recipes in this chapter can be baked in bundts, loaves, tube pans, 9x13-inch pans, or muffin cups.

- Bake in paperware baking pans.

- Since consumers are buying smaller-sized products, also consider selling half cakes or small loaves.

Tips for Handling:

- With bundt pans, we flip the baked product over. The flat top becomes the bottom, while the bottom decorative design becomes the top. With tube pans, the tops remain as baked. When you are thinking about how to finish your product, remember that a streusel only works for the plain tube-shaped pan.

- To stop baked goods from sticking to their plate, first sprinkle granulated sugar on the plate, which soaks up excess moisture.

- After finishing, all cakes must be kept well wrapped.

Variations:

- For pound cakes, add streusel or nuts before baking.

- For all recipes, finish with a light dusting of confectioners' sugar, glaze, or string icing.

- Use pound or bundt cake recipes to make cupcakes. Ice with your favorite buttercream.

Carrot Bundt Cakes

Carrot Bundt Cake

Fine-grained and moist, the fresh ginger gives this cake a punch.

Yield: 10-cup Bundt pan

- 1 cup oil
- 2 cups sugar
- 3 large eggs
- ½ cup applesauce
- 2 teaspoons vanilla
- 2 cups grated carrots
- 2 tablespoons fresh grated ginger
- 1 ½ cups whole wheat pastry flour
- 1 ½ cups all-purpose flour
- 2 teaspoons baking soda
- 1 teaspoon salt
- 1 tablespoon cinnamon
- 1 cup raisins, optional

1. Preheat oven to 350° F. and grease baking pan.

2. Mix together oil, sugar, eggs, applesauce, and vanilla in a large bowl. Stir in carrots and ginger.

3. In a separate bowl, stir together both flours, baking soda, salt, and cinnamon. Stir into the wet ingredients. Mix in the raisins, if using.

4. Pour batter into prepared pan and bake 60 to 70 minutes, until the top feels firm when gently pressed and a toothpick inserted in the center comes out clean.

5. Let the cake cool for 10 to 15 minutes and turn upside down onto a serving plate or cake circle. Keeps up to five days at room temperature.

INSIDER TIPS
- Add fresh chopped apples or pears in season.
- This recipe makes excellent carrot cupcakes.
- After baking, glaze or sprinkle with sifted confectioners' sugar.

CATEGORIES
- Whole grain
- Dairy free
- Nut free

Cinnamon Crown Bundt Cake

This cake is from my Aunt Ethel's recipe box, and one of the first bundt cakes I made for sale. It's a moist cake with a beautiful swirl.

Yield: 12-cup Bundt pan

- ½ pound (2 sticks) butter
- 2 cups sugar
- 3 large eggs
- 1 tablespoon vanilla
- 3 cups flour
- 1 tablespoon baking powder
- ½ teaspoon salt
- 1 cup milk
- ½ cup applesauce
- ½ cup quick oats
- ½ cup brown sugar
- 2 teaspoons cinnamon

1. Preheat oven to 350° F. and grease baking pan.
2. Beat butter and sugar together in a large bowl. Add eggs and vanilla, beating until combined.
3. In a separate bowl stir together flour, baking powder, and salt. Alternately add the dry ingredients and milk until completely combined.
4. Pour half the batter into a bowl and stir in the applesauce, oats, sugar, and cinnamon. Pour this batter into the bottom of the prepared bundt pan, then pour remaining batter on top. You do not need to swirl since the cake will form a pretty pattern as it bakes.
5. Bake 60 to 70 minutes, until the top feels firm when gently pressed and a toothpick inserted in the center comes out clean.
6. Let cake cool 10 to15 minutes. Turn upside down onto a serving plate or cake circle. Keeps up to five days at room temperature.

INSIDER TIPS
- After baking, use cinnamon glaze (Chapter 15) or sift confectioners' sugar over top.
- Add 1 cup finely chopped peeled apple to the applesauce-oat mixture.

CATEGORIES
- Nut free

Double Raspberry Pound Cake

I created this pound cake for a special order. It was so good, with fresh raspberries and raspberry liqueur, it became part of our seasonal repertoire.

Yield: 12-cup tube pan

- 1 pound (4 sticks) butter
- 3 cups sugar
- 6 large eggs
- ½ teaspoon vanilla
- 4 cups flour
- 1 teaspoon salt
- ½ teaspoon baking soda
- ¾ cup sour cream
- ¼ cup raspberry liqueur
- 1 cup fresh or frozen raspberries (do not thaw)

1. Preheat oven to 325° F. and grease pan.

2. Cream butter and sugar in a large bowl, then add eggs and vanilla and beat for another minute.

3. In a medium bowl stir together flour, salt, and baking soda. In a measuring cup combine sour cream and liqueur, then alternately add flour and liquid to the butter mixture, starting and ending with the dry ingredients. The batter will be very thick.

4. Scoop batter into prepared pan, then scatter raspberries on top and lightly press in. Bake 60 to 75 minutes, until the cake feels firm when gently pressed and a toothpick inserted near the center comes out dry.

5. Cool for 15 or 20 minutes before turning out of pan. Keeps five days at room temperature.

INSIDER TIPS
- For Peach Melba Pound Cake, add 1 cup finely diced peaches, ¼ cup extra flour, and finish with a raspberry glaze (Chapter 15).
- Bake in a 9x13-inch pan or as cupcakes, and frost with raspberry buttercream (Chapter 15).

CATEGORIES
- Nut free

Five Flavor Pound Cake

Five Flavor Pound Cake is a favorite in many parts of the U.S. Aunt Ethel said that butter, coconut milk, and five different extracts made her pound cake seven flavors. But I still used the accepted name.

Yield: 12-cup tube pan

- ¾ pound (3 sticks) butter
- 2 ½ cups sugar
- 5 large eggs
- 3 ¾ cups flour
- ½ teaspoon baking powder
- ⅛ teaspoon baking soda
- ½ teaspoon salt
- 1 cup coconut milk
- 1 teaspoon vanilla extract
- ½ teaspoon lemon extract
- ½ teaspoon orange extract
- ¼ teaspoon almond extract
- ¼ teaspoon rum extract

1. Preheat oven to 350° F. and grease pan.

2. Cream butter and sugar in a large bowl, then add eggs and beat for another minute.

3. In a medium bowl stir together flour, baking powder, baking soda, and salt. In a measuring cup, combine coconut milk and extracts. Alternately add flour and liquid to the butter mixture, starting and ending with the dry ingredients. The batter will be very thick.

4. Scoop batter into prepared pan and bake 30 minutes. Turn heat down to 325° F. and bake another 35 to 45 minutes, until the cake feels firm when gently pressed and a toothpick inserted near the center comes out dry.

5. Cool for 15 or 20 minutes before turning out of pan. Keeps five days at room temperature.

INSIDER TIPS

- Instead of five flavors, add or delete extracts. If adding other extracts (try butter, coconut, or brandy) use ¼ to 1 teaspoon extract per flavor.
- Dust with confectioners' sugar.
- If you prefer a cooked glaze instead of confectioners' sugar, boil ½ cup water and ¼ cup sugar for 1 minute. Stir in ½ teaspoon each of all the extracts and pour over warm cake.

CATEGORIES

- Nut free

Marble Bundt Cake

Another winning recipe from my Aunt Ethel, this beautiful fine-grained cake has a delicious flavor and adapts well to many shapes and sizes.

Yield: 12-cup Bundt pan

- 1 cup (6-ounce) bag semi-sweet chocolate chips
- ¼ pound (1 stick) butter, melted
- ½ cup oil
- 2 cups granulated sugar
- 4 large eggs
- 1 tablespoon vanilla extract
- 1 teaspoon almond extract
- 1 cup milk
- 3 ½ cups flour
- 2 ½ teaspoons baking powder
- ½ teaspoon baking soda
- ½ teaspoon salt

1. Melt chips in a small bowl and set aside to cool.

2. Preheat oven to 350° F. and grease pan.

3. In a large bowl combine the melted butter, oil, sugar, eggs, and extracts. Stir in milk.

4. In a medium bowl stir together flour, baking powder, baking soda, and salt. Add to the butter mixture, and beat until thoroughly mixed. The batter will be thick.

5. Pour about 2 cups of batter into another bowl (a 4-cup measure is perfect for this step) and add the chocolate, combining well.

6. Pour vanilla batter into the prepared pan and drop chocolate batter on top. Gently swirl together, but don't swirl too much or you will lose the effect. Bake 50 to 60 minutes, until the cake pulls away from the sides of the pan and the top feels firm when a finger is pressed gently on top.

7. Cool for 15 minutes, then turn onto a cake board or platter. Keeps several days at room temperature.

INSIDER TIPS

- Glaze with a semi-sweet chocolate icing (Chapter 15).
- Grease large muffin pans (do not use paper liners) and fill halfway. After baking, turn upside down, cool, and glaze the flat top with chocolate.
- To make a sheet cake, bake in a (greased) 9x13-inch pan. Spread all chocolate batter on bottom of pan, refrigerate for several minutes, and spread apricot jam over batter. Carefully spread vanilla batter over jam. After baking, ice with chocolate buttercream.

CATEGORIES

- Nut free

Old Fashioned Pound Cake

This multi-purpose pound cake has a thick crusty top and a mild citrus/vanilla flavor.

Yield: 12-cup tube pan

- ½ pound (2 sticks) butter
- ½ cup vegetable oil
- 3 cups sugar
- 5 large eggs
- 1 teaspoon vanilla extract
- 1 teaspoon lemon extract
- 4 cups flour
- ½ teaspoon baking powder
- ½ teaspoon salt
- 1 cup milk
- ¼ cup rum (or use more milk)

1. Preheat oven to 350° F. and grease pan.

2. Beat together butter, oil, and sugar in a large bowl. Add eggs and extracts, beating until thoroughly combined.

3. In a separate bowl, stir together flour, baking powder, and salt. In another cup combine the milk and rum. Alternately add these to the butter mixture, beginning and ending with the dry ingredients.

4. Scrape batter into pan and bake 55 to 75 minutes. If cake is getting too dark on top, turn oven down to 325° F. When done, the top should be golden brown and feel firm when gently pressed. Keeps several days at room temperature.

INSIDER TIPS
- Substitute any favorite liquor for the rum.
- Add 1 cup (6-ounce) bag mini chocolate chips.
- Use for cupcakes and all occasion cakes.
- Slice and dip one end of each piece into melted chocolate.

CATEGORIES
- Nut free

Orange Poppyseed Bundt Cake

Fast and easy with an attractive split around the top, this cake adapts well to many flavors. Recipe courtesy of my mom.

Yield: 10-cup Bundt pan

- 1 cup oil
- 1 ¾ cups sugar
- 4 large eggs
- 1 teaspoon vanilla extract
- 1 teaspoon orange extract
- 1 ¼ cups orange juice
- 3 ¼ cups flour
- $^1/_3$ cup poppyseeds
- 1 teaspoon baking powder
- ½ teaspoon baking soda
- ½ teaspoon salt

1. Preheat oven to 350° F. and grease pan.

2. In a large bowl beat oil, sugar, eggs, extracts, and orange juice.

3. In a separate bowl, combine flour, poppy seeds, baking powder, baking soda, and salt. Add to the wet ingredients and mix well.

4. Pour into prepared pan and bake 45 to 55 minutes. Cake is done when it pulls away from the sides of the pan, has a split along the top, and passes the toothpick test. Keeps five days at room temperature.

INSIDER TIPS
- Quick fix
- For an Orange Bundt Cake, delete poppy seeds.
- Add 1 cup finely chopped fresh seasonal fruit and ¼ cup additional flour.
- After baking, apply vanilla or orange glaze (Chapter 15).

CATEGORIES
- Dairy free
- Nut free

Red Velvet Pound Cake

Red Velvet is a southern favorite with a touch of cocoa and lots of red food coloring. Instead of coloring, I used a red-tinted nut liqueur and it became an instant bestseller. Customers preferred a chocolate glaze over the traditional cream cheese topping.

Yield: 10-cup tube pan

- ½ pound (2 sticks) butter
- 1 ½ cups sugar
- 3 large eggs
- ½ teaspoon vanilla
- 2 ½ cups flour
- 2 tablespoons cocoa
- ¼ teaspoon baking soda
- ¼ teaspoon baking powder
- ½ teaspoon salt
- 2 tablespoons red food color, optional
- ½ cup red nut liqueur (may substitute milk but the flavor will change)

Chocolate Glaze
- 1 tablespoon butter, melted
- 2 tablespoons cocoa
- 3 tablespoons milk
- 1 teaspoon vanilla extract
- 1 cup confectioners' sugar

1. Preheat oven to 350° F. and grease pan.

2. Cream butter and sugar in a large bowl. Add eggs and vanilla and beat another minute.

3. In a medium bowl stir together flour, cocoa, baking soda, baking powder, and salt. Measure liqueur (or other liquid) and add red color, if using. Alternately add flour and liqueur to the butter mixture, starting and ending with the dry ingredients. Batter will be very thick.

4. Scoop into prepared pan and bake 50 to 60 minutes, until the cake feels firm when gently pressed and a toothpick inserted near the center comes out dry.

5. Cool for 15 or 20 minutes before turning out of pan. Glaze when cool. Mix all glaze ingredients in the order listed and pour over top of cake. Keeps five days at room temperature.

INSIDER TIPS

- Bake in a 9x13-inch pan and frost with a cream cheese icing (Chapter 15).
- Add 1 cup (6-ounce) bag mini chocolate chips.
- For Blue Velvet Pound Cake, delete cocoa and use milk for liquid. Be daring and add 2 tablespoons or more blue color. Hum "Blue Velvet" while baking. Use cream cheese icing.
- For Red, White, and Blue Pound Cake, delete cocoa and use milk for liquid. Divide batter in thirds. See above for red and blue. Pour into pan and gently swirl colors. Hum national anthem. Great for 4th of July celebrations. Must fly American flag while baking.

Triple Chocolate Pound Cake

One of our best sellers, I developed this recipe for my chocoholic customers. They love its soft-grained texture with a nice hit of chocolate.

Yield: 12-cup tube pan

- ¾ pound (3 sticks) butter
- 2 ½ cups brown sugar
- 5 large eggs
- 2 teaspoons vanilla
- 3 ¼ cups flour
- ½ cup cocoa
- ½ teaspoon baking powder
- ¼ teaspoon baking soda
- ½ teaspoon salt
- ¾ cup milk
- ¼ cup coffee liqueur or milk
- 1 cup (6-ounce) bag mini chocolate chips

Chocolate Glaze
- 1 tablespoon butter, melted
- 2 tablespoons cocoa
- 3 tablespoons milk
- 1 teaspoon vanilla extract
- 1 cup confectioners' sugar

1. Preheat oven to 325° F. and grease pan.

2. Cream butter and sugar in a large bowl, then beat in eggs and vanilla.

3. In a medium bowl stir together flour, cocoa, baking powder, baking soda, and salt. In a separate bowl combine milk and liqueur then alternately add dry and liquid to the butter mixture, starting and ending with dry ingredients. The batter will be very thick.

4. Scoop batter into pan. Bake 60 to 75 minutes, until cake feels firm when gently pressed and a toothpick inserted near the center comes out dry.

5. Cool 15 or 20 minutes before turning out of pan. Glaze when cool. Mix all glaze ingredients in order listed and pour over top of cake. Keeps up to five days.

INSIDER TIPS

- Add 1 cup (6-ounce bag) white chocolate or milk chocolate chips.
- For Chocolate Raspberry Pound Cake, after batter is in pan place 1 cup fresh or frozen berries on top of batter and press in.
- Bake in mini-muffin cups for Chocolate Pound Cake "Shots."

CATEGORIES

- Nut free

Tunnel of Fudge Bundt Cake

This is my scratch-made version of the famous bake-off winner. But here, nuts are optional. This recipe also makes great brownies.

Yield: 12-cup Bundt pan

- 1 pound (4 sticks) butter
- 2 cups granulated sugar
- 2 cups confectioners' sugar
- 6 large eggs
- 1 tablespoon vanilla
- 2 ½ cups flour
- ¾ cup cocoa
- ½ teaspoon baking powder
- ½ teaspoon salt
- 1 ½ cups chopped nuts, optional

Chocolate Glaze
- 1 cup powdered sugar
- $^1/_3$ cup cocoa
- 2 tablespoons softened butter
- 2 tablespoons milk
- 1 teaspoon vanilla

1. Preheat oven to 350° F. and grease pan.

2. In a large mixer bowl cream butter, both sugars, eggs, and vanilla.

3. In a separate bowl combine flour, cocoa, baking powder, and salt. Stir until there are no lumps of cocoa and add to the butter/sugar mixture. Beat until combined. Add nuts, if using. The batter will be thick.

4. Pour into prepared pan and bake for 1 hour, then turn heat down to 325° F. and bake another 15 minutes, or until the top looks firm. If your oven has too much bottom heat, place the pan on a cookie sheet. To create the fudgy tunnel, this cake needs to be slightly underbaked. Getting the bake time right takes some practice. When I'm in doubt, I let it bake a few minutes longer, since not enough baking will result in a cake that falls apart.

5. Cool before turning onto a plate or cake circle. Mix all glaze ingredients in the order listed and pour over top of cake. Keeps up to five days at room temperature.

INSIDER TIPS

- For brownies, use a deep 9x13x2-inch pan.
- Instead of glaze, dust with confectioners' sugar.

Chapter 12

Scones, Biscuits, and Crackers

Scones and biscuits are traditional breakfast fare, perfect with a cup of tea or coffee. My bakery had a daily breakfast special and always paired our coffee with the scone or biscuit flavor of the week. On weekends we sold them boxed by the half-dozen with a fruited butter spread, and during the spring and summer months we used them in shortcakes with seasonal fruit.

During the winter months, biscuits accompanied a bowl of our homemade soup. When we were out of biscuits, customers received crackers. This led to customer requests for purchasing these savory treats to take home. We sold the crackers in half-pound and pound bags. In this chapter I've included the two best-selling cracker recipes.

So what *is* the difference between biscuits and scones? Depending upon whom you ask, scones are usually made with egg and are sweeter than biscuits, which are generally plain. The second difference is flavor. Scones can be any flavor and have additions, but biscuits are usually plain. For most customers, however, the main difference between a scone and a biscuit is the shape. Scones are triangular, biscuits are round. That's probably the most important distinction when baking for sale. And with most customers, you want to give them what is familiar and expected.

Another difference is that biscuits appear to have originated in the United States, with several regions claiming them as their own. Scones originated in Europe with Britain, Scotland, and Ireland all claiming origin. Regardless of differences, your goal is simply to make your customers happy.

Tips for Baking:
* Line cookie sheets with parchment or non-stick mats.
* Brush with egg wash for a shiny top.
* Sprinkle sweet scones or biscuits with coarse sugar before baking.
* For softer scones and biscuits, bake close together with sides touching.

Tips for Handling:
* To make biscuit or scone dough using a mixer, add and mix your dry ingredients first. Then drop in all the small pieces of fat and mix briefly

by hand to cover the fat with flour. Briefly turn the mixer on until the fat is evenly distributed. You might need to help this along by stopping the mixer and separating any large pieces. Watch carefully! When you see the dough starting to form a ball, it's done.

- If incorporating fresh fruits into dough, handle the dough gently to avoid mashing the fruits, which will look unsightly.

- Let baked goods cool before wrapping.

- Let crackers bake and dry thoroughly before packaging.

Variations:
- Incorporate fresh or dried herbs into cracker or biscuit dough. I particularly like dill, rosemary, or basil.

- Add chopped dried fruits to any dough, particularly cranberries, raisins, or dates.

- For cobbler topping, drop any scone or biscuit dough onto hot fruit and bake until golden.

Cinnamon Buns from the Biscuit Dry Mix

Biscuit Dry Mix

This multi-purpose biscuit mix makes production schedules easier.

Yield: approximately 6 ½ cups mix, enough for 24+ biscuits

- 4 ½ cups flour
- 2 tablespoons baking powder
- ½ teaspoon baking soda
- 2 teaspoons salt
- ¼ cup sugar
- 1 cup shortening

1. Mix together flour, baking powder, baking soda, salt, and sugar in a large bowl.

2. Cut in the shortening with a knife, pastry cutter, or fingers. When fully mixed and crumbly, store in an airtight container, in a cool dry location.

3. Keeps up to three months.

To bake:

1. Preheat oven to 400° F. and prepare cookie sheet with a liner.

2. For 1 dozen medium *drop biscuits*, scoop 3 cups mix into a medium bowl. Combine with ¾ cup liquid (milk, buttermilk, orange juice, or water). Drop from a scoop onto the baking sheet.

3. For 1 dozen *rolled biscuits*, scoop 3 cups mix into a medium bowl. Combine with ²/₃ cup liquid (milk, buttermilk, orange juice, or water). Roll out on a floured board and cut into the traditional biscuit shape.

4. Bake 12 to 18 minutes, or until a light brown. Biscuits keep for two days.

INSIDER TIPS
- Quick fix
- Recipe may be scaled up to any amount. I use a large stockpot and mix by hand.
- For a savory biscuit, reduce or delete sugar.
- Sell as a dry mix and include baking directions.
- Can be used to replace boxed biscuit mix recipes, including "impossible pie" recipes.
- For cheese and herb biscuits, add ½ cup grated cheese and approximately 1 tablespoon fresh herbs, or 2 teaspoons for dried herbs.

- For fruit cobbler, use drop biscuit recipe and spoon over hot fruit filling. Bake at 400° F. until biscuits are golden brown and fruit filling bubbles.
- For cinnamon buns, use rolled biscuit dough above, and roll into rectangle. Brush with melted butter and sprinkle with cinnamon sugar. Roll up and cut into ½-inch slices. Bake at 400° F. for 10 to 15 minutes. Glaze when cool.
- For savory pinwheels, roll dough into a large rectangle, brush with melted butter, and use leftover meat, casserole, or vegetable as the filling. Bake at 400° F. for 10 to 15 minutes. Serve with a sauce (canned or home-made) if desired.
- For pot pies, make rolled biscuit dough above, and use as top crust over any filling. Bake at 400° F. until deep golden brown and the fruit filling bubbles.

CATEGORIES

- Nut free
- Egg free
- Vegan

Champagne Crackers

I wondered what I was going to do with the last of that champagne. These crackers were an immediate hit!

Yield: 24-36 crackers

- 2 cups flour
- $^1/_3$ cup sugar
- ½ teaspoon baking powder
- ½ teaspoon baking soda
- ¼ teaspoon salt
- 6 tablespoons (¾ stick) butter
- $^2/_3$ cup champagne

1. Preheat oven to 375° F. and prepare cookie sheets with liners.

2. Mix together flour, sugar, baking powder, baking soda, and salt in a medium bowl.

3. Cut in butter and add enough champagne to form a ball of dough. Knead lightly.

4. Roll out and cut into squares or use cookie cutters. Prick crackers with a fork.

5. Bake 20 to 30 minutes until light golden brown around edges. Keeps several weeks.

INSIDER TIPS
- Substitute any white wine for the champagne.
- Before baking, sprinkle tops with sesame, poppy, or caraway seeds.

CATEGORIES
- Egg free
- Nut free

Coffee Scones

These scones were inspired by a coffee-flavored biscuit recipe I found in a community cookbook.

Yield: 8 scones

- 2 ¼ cups flour
- ½ cup brown sugar
- 1 tablespoon instant or espresso coffee powder
- 1 teaspoon baking powder
- ¼ teaspoon baking soda
- ¼ teaspoon salt
- ¼ pound (1 stick) cold butter
- ½ cup milk
- ¼ cup cold coffee
- 1 teaspoon vanilla
- 1 teaspoon raw or granulated sugar

1. Preheat oven to 375° F. and prepare cookie sheet with liner.

2. Mix together flour, sugar, coffee powder, baking powder, baking soda, and salt in a medium bowl.

3. Cut butter into thin slices and add to the dry ingredients. Use your mixer paddle or a knife to combine. When butter becomes small pea-sized pieces, pour in milk, coffee, and vanilla. Mix until dough holds together.

4. Place dough on prepared cookie sheet and form into a ½-inch thick round, approximately 8-inches across. Sprinkle top with sugar, cut into 8 wedges, and separate with at least 1-inch between each piece. Bake 25 to 35 minutes until a medium golden brown. Keeps two days.

INSIDER TIPS
- Add 1 cup (6-ounce bag) chocolate chips before adding liquid.
- Roll out and cut into round biscuits for raspberry shortcakes.
- Serve warm scones with chocolate hazelnut spread.

CATEGORIES
- Egg free
- Nut free

Cream Scones

The Scots made traditional scones from oats, shaped them into triangles, and baked them on a griddle. Today you can find round and square scones, usually oven-baked. You have great leeway in varying this basic scone recipe by adding a wide range of dried fruits, nuts, sweets, and spices.

Yield: 8 large or 12 medium scones

- 2 cups flour
- 2 tablespoons sugar, plus additional for sprinkling tops
- 1 tablespoon baking powder
- ½ teaspoon baking soda
- ½ teaspoon salt
- 6 tablespoons (¾ stick) cold butter, cut into pieces
- ½ cup dried or fresh fruit, such as cranberries, apples, apricots, or dates
- ½ cup heavy cream or half 'n half, plus additional for brushing scone tops
- 1 large egg
- 1 teaspoon vanilla, orange, or lemon extract; or ½ teaspoon almond extract

1. Preheat oven to 400° F. and prepare cookie sheets with liner.

2. Stir together flour, sugar, baking powder, baking soda, and salt in a medium bowl.

3. Using your mixer or a knife, cut in butter until the ingredients are pea-sized pieces. Stir in dried or fresh fruit.

4. In a separate bowl stir together cream, egg, and extract. Mix this liquid into the dry ingredients just until it forms a soft dough. Add more liquid if too dry and crumbly or more flour if too wet.

5. Scrape dough onto a lightly floured surface and knead gently for 30 seconds until it's no longer sticky. If you have included fresh fruits, knead carefully to avoid mashing.

6. Pat into a ½-inch thick round. Score the top into 8 or 12 pieces, brush top with milk or cream, and sprinkle with sugar. Cut all the way through. Separate scones and place on baking sheet.

7. Bake 15 to 18 minutes, or until golden. Keeps two days.

INSIDER TIPS

- Suggested combinations: add ½ cup each for the following combinations, Cranberry Coconut, Carrot Raisin, Date and Walnut.
- For savory scones, use only 1 tablespoon sugar and no extract. Add ½ cup fresh or frozen finely chopped vegetables (onions or green peppers work particularly well), and 1 tablespoon fresh or 1 teaspoon dried herbs such as dill or basil. You could also add ½ cup shredded cheese or small pieces of ham or cooked bacon.

CATEGORIES

- Nut free

Multi-Grain Crackers

Better than any factory made crackers because of the real homemade flavor and texture.

Yield: 36-40 medium crackers

- 1 cup whole wheat pastry flour
- ½ cup rye flour
- ½ cup all-purpose flour
- 1 teaspoon baking powder
- ¼ teaspoon baking soda
- ⅛ teaspoon salt
- ¼ cup (½ stick) butter, cold
- ¾ cup water
- optional toppings such as sesame seed, poppyseed, caraway seeds, salt, and/or cracked pepper

1. Preheat oven to 375° F. and prepare cookie sheets with liners.

2. Mix together whole wheat, rye, and all-purpose flour in a medium bowl. Stir in baking powder, baking soda, and salt.

3. Using your mixer or knife, cut in butter and add enough water to form a dough. Knead briefly.

4. Roll out and cut into traditional squares or cookie cutter shapes. Prick with a fork and bake plain or sprinkle with your choice of toppings.

5. Bake 20 to 30 minutes until edges are brown and crackers are thoroughly dry. Keeps one month.

INSIDER TIPS
- Substitute any wholegrain flour for all-purpose and add 1 or 2 tablespoons extra water.
- Use juice or brewed tea instead of water.
- Sell packaged with a butter herb spread.

CATEGORIES
- Whole grain
- Egg free
- Nut free

Simple Scones

No cutting in butter when heavy cream is substituted for the butter.

Yield: 8 medium scones

- 2 cups flour, plus additional for kneading
- 1 tablespoon baking powder
- 2 tablespoons sugar
- ½ teaspoon salt
- ½ cup chopped dried fruit, such as raisins or cranberries, optional
- 1 ½ cups heavy cream

1. Preheat oven to 400° F. and prepare cookie sheet with liner.

2. Mix together flour, baking powder, sugar, and salt in a medium bowl. Mix in dried fruit, if using.

3. Pour in heavy cream and stir until almost thoroughly mixed. Dough will hold together but appear ragged. Knead several turns, using extra flour, until it forms a ball. Flour more if too sticky.

4. Place ball of dough on cookie sheet and flatten to approximately 1-inch thick. Brush top with milk or water and cut into 8 wedges. Separate and move pieces at least 2 inches apart.

5. Bake 15 to 20 minutes, until tops are golden brown. Keeps two days.

INSIDER TIPS
- Quick fix
- For a sweeter scone, add 1 more tablespoon sugar.
- For a savory scone, delete sugar and add ½ cup each grated cheese and chopped veggies.
- Before baking, tops can be sprinkled with sugar or herbs.

CATEGORIES
- Egg free
- Nut free

Super Fast Biscuits

Shhhh, don't tell anyone. These are made with oil for a super quick fix product.

Yield: 12 medium biscuits

- 2 ¼ cups flour
- 1 tablespoon baking powder
- ¼ teaspoon salt
- ½ cup oil
- ¾ cup milk or water

1. Preheat oven to 400° F. and prepare cookie sheet with liner.

2. Stir together flour, baking powder, and salt in a medium bowl.

3. In a measuring cup, combine oil and milk, then pour into dry ingredients. Mix until dough holds together.

4. Divide dough into 12 equal-sized pieces. Using extra flour on the counter, roll into balls and place on prepared tray. Flatten slightly.

5. Bake 15 to 20 minutes until a medium golden brown. Keeps two days.

INSIDER TIPS
- Quick fix
- For simple rolled biscuits, dust counter with flour and form a square approximately 6x8-inches. Cut into 12 pieces.
- Add 1 cup chopped seasonal produce, either fruit or veggies.

CATEGORIES
- Egg free
- Nut free

Sweet Apple Biscuits

Here's another easy-to-mix recipe.

Yield: 12 medium biscuits

- 2 cups flour
- ½ cup sugar
- 1 teaspoon baking powder
- ½ teaspoon baking soda
- ½ teaspoon salt
- 1 large egg, beaten
- 1 cup sour cream
- I medium apple, diced, with or without peel

1. Preheat oven to 400° F. and prepare cookie sheet with liner.

2. Mix together flour, sugar, baking powder, baking soda, and salt in a medium bowl.

3. Add egg and sour cream, mixing lightly. Add apples and blend gently. The dough should be thick and wet.

4. Scoop by ¼ cupfuls onto cookie sheet and bake 15 to 20 minutes, until tops are medium golden brown. Keeps two days.

INSIDER TIPS
- Quick fix
- Substitute 1 cup chopped seasonal fruit. Pears, peaches, or plums work particularly well.
- Add 1 teaspoon cinnamon.

CATEGORIES
- Nut free

Chapter 13

Sweet Quickbreads

Quickbreads are batters that can be baked immediately, without the rising period yeast doughs demand. The leavening action occurs from chemical leaveners, most often baking powder or baking soda. These loaves are eaten sliced and buttered, but sometimes customers prefer cream cheese, jams, or both.

Tea cakes are usually sweeter than loaves, served at tea time, and can be eaten without utensils.

As with pound cakes and bundt cakes, the trend is toward smaller products. Bake these in smaller loaf pans and let customers know you will take orders for larger sizes. For venues where people may consume the quickbreads immediately, such as a farmers' market or deli, sell slices of breads either plain or buttered, and pre-wrapped. Individual slices are a nice way to get customers to (buy their own) sample. Once they have tasted your breads they will be more willing to order larger loaves for special occasions.

Zucchini Bread

Tips for baking:
- All recipes in the muffin chapter may be baked in loaf form.

- Loaves need a long bake time, so if the tops appear too dark, turn heat down 25° F. for the last 15 or 20 minutes.

- Loaves are done when they pull away from the sides of the pan, have a split along the top, and pass the toothpick test (the federal no-cake-left-behind rule applies here, also).

Tips for handling:
- Let cool at least 15 minutes before removing from pan.

- Buy disposable loaf pans in paperware or aluminum. Baking in these pans means less clean-up.

Variations:
- Before baking, sprinkle top with nuts or streusel (Chapter 15).

- After loaves are cool, top with confectioners' sugar, glaze, or string icing (Chapter 15).

Applesauce Loaf

This loaf is not too sweet, with a pretty marbled appearance.

Yield: 1 9x5-inch loaf pan

- ½ cup oil
- ¾ cup applesauce
- 1 cup brown sugar
- 1 large egg
- 2 teaspoons vanilla
- 2 ½ cups flour
- 1 teaspoon baking soda
- ¾ teaspoon baking powder
- ½ teaspoon salt
- 1 small finely chopped apple, with peel
- 2 teaspoons cinnamon
- ¼ teaspoon nutmeg
- ¼ teaspoon allspice
- 2 teaspoons cinnamon sugar

1. Preheat oven to 350° F. and grease loaf pan.
2. Combine oil, applesauce, sugar, egg, and vanilla in a medium bowl.
3. In another bowl stir together flour, baking soda, baking powder, and salt. Add to the wet ingredients and stir until combined.
4. Pour 1 cup of batter into a small bowl and stir in apple, cinnamon, nutmeg, and allspice.
5. Pour plain batter into prepared baking pan. Pour apple batter along the length of the loaf. Swirl slightly. Sprinkle 2 teaspoons of cinnamon sugar over the top.
6. Bake 50 to 60 minutes. Loaf is done when a toothpick inserted into the center comes out dry, or the top of the bread feels firm when lightly pressed. Keeps several days at room temperature.

INSIDER TIPS
- Substitute 1 small pear for the apple, add ½ teaspoon ground ginger.
- For coffeecakes, use an 8x8-inch pan and spread spiced batter on the bottom. Add plain batter and sprinkle with streusel (Chapter 15). Bake for 35 to 40 minutes.

CATEGORIES
- Dairy free
- Nut free

Avocado Tea Cake

A friend (long-lost but not forgotten) gave me this recipe when we visited her family in Texas. It's an unusual tea cake, more expensive than most, but a great seller when used to promote an ethnic event.

Yield: 1 8x4-inch loaf pan

- 1 cup mashed avocado (approximately 1 large)
- ½ cup oil
- ¾ cup sugar
- 1 large egg
- ½ cup milk
- 1 tablespoon lemon juice
- 2 cups flour
- 1 teaspoon baking soda
- ½ teaspoon baking powder
- 1 teaspoon cinnamon
- ¼ teaspoon salt
- ½ cup chopped dates
- 1 cup chopped nuts, optional

1. Preheat oven to 350° F. and grease loaf pan.

2. Stir together avocado, oil, sugar, egg, milk, and lemon juice in a medium bowl.

3. In separate bowl mix together flour, baking soda, baking powder, cinnamon, and salt. Add to dry ingredients and mix well. Stir in dates and nuts (if using).

4. Pour into pan and bake 50 to 60 minutes, until a finger pressed gently on top leaves no imprint. Keeps several days at room temperature.

INSIDER TIPS
- Bake as mini-muffins and finish with a heavy dusting of confectioners' sugar.
- Instead of dates use currants or chopped raisins.

Banana Bread

This recipe, from my mom, has enough sugar to qualify as cake. It was always one of our best selling loaves. Must be all the sugar.

Yield: 1 8x4-inch loaf pan

- ¼ pound (1 stick) butter
- 1¼ cups sugar
- 2 large eggs
- 3 small or 2 large bananas, mashed (about 1 cup)
- ¼ cup sour cream
- 2 teaspoons vanilla
- 2 cups flour
- 1 teaspoon baking soda
- ½ teaspoon salt
- ½ cup walnuts, optional

1. Preheat oven to 350° F. and grease pan.

2. Cream butter with sugar in a medium bowl. Add eggs, bananas, sour cream, and vanilla. Mix until well blended.

3. Add flour, baking soda, and salt and mix until no flour is visible. The batter should be thick. Add nuts, if using. Scrape batter into prepared pan.

4. Bake 45 to 55 minutes. If it looks like it's getting too dark but needs more baking (the split will appear wet), turn temperature down to 325° F. Keeps several days at room temperature.

INSIDER TIPS
- Sprinkle top with a few chopped walnuts.
- Add 1 cup (6-ounce) bag milk chocolate chips.
- After baking, drizzle top with melted chocolate.

Basic Sour Cream Sweetbread

This basic loaf adapts well to different flavors and additions.

Yield: 1 8x4-inch loaf pan

- ¼ pound (1 stick) butter
- 1 cup sugar
- 2 large eggs
- 2 teaspoons vanilla
- 1 cup sour cream
- 2 ¾ cups flour
- 1 teaspoon baking soda
- 1 teaspoon baking powder
- ½ teaspoon salt

1. Preheat oven to 350° F. and grease baking pan.

2. Beat together butter and sugar in a medium bowl. Add eggs, vanilla, and sour cream, beating until thoroughly combined.

3. In a separate bowl, mix together flour, baking soda, baking powder, and salt. Add to the butter mixture. Beat until thoroughly mixed.

4. Pour into pan and bake 60 to 70 minutes, until a toothpick inserted into the center comes out dry, or the top feels firm when lightly pressed. Keeps several days at room temperature.

INSIDER TIPS

- Quick fix
- I prefer the richness of full-fat sour cream but fat-free yogurt also works.
- Substitute 1 teaspoon lemon or almond extract for 1 teaspoon of vanilla.
- Excellent for seasonal fruits. Add 1-2 cups any fresh chopped fruit, such as apples, plums, or nectarines.
- Add streusel (Chapter 15) before baking.

CATEGORIES

- Nut free

Date Nut Bread

Another great recipe from baker Saraly. This loaf is excellent thinly sliced and spread with cream cheese.

Yield: 1 8x4-inch loaf pan

- 8 ounces dates, chopped
- 1 cup hot water
- 1 ¼ teaspoons baking soda
- ¼ cup oil
- ¾ cup sugar
- 1 large egg
- 1 teaspoon vanilla or orange extract
- ¼ teaspoon salt
- 1 ¼ cups whole wheat pastry flour
- 1 ¼ cups all-purpose flour
- ½ cup chopped walnuts

1. Soak dates in water until soft, at least one hour, then add baking soda and set aside.

2. Preheat oven to 350° F. and grease pan.

3. Combine oil, sugar, egg, extract, and salt in a medium bowl. Stir in dates and water.

4. Mix in the flours. The batter should be thick. Stir in walnuts.

5. Bake 45 to 55 minutes, until a finger pressed lightly on top leaves no imprint. Keeps one week at room temperature.

INSIDER TIPS
- Soak dates in orange juice instead of water.
- Use pecans instead of walnuts.
- Sprinkle top with ¼ cup finely chopped nuts and dust with confectioners' sugar.

CATEGORIES
- Whole grain
- Dairy free

Harvest Loaf

This recipe began as a carrot cake experiment, then morphed into a dark moist loaf chock full of dried fruits.

Yield: 1 8x4-inch loaf pan

- 1 ¼ cups sugar
- ½ cup oil
- 2 large eggs
- ½ cup applesauce
- 1 teaspoon vanilla
- 1 ¼ cups whole wheat pastry flour
- 1 cup all-purpose flour
- 1 teaspoon baking soda
- 2 teaspoons cinnamon
- ½ teaspoon salt
- 2 cups total any combination of raisins, chopped dates, coconut, or dried cranberries

1. Preheat oven to 350° F. and grease pan.

2. Combine sugar, oil, eggs, applesauce, and vanilla in a medium bowl.

3. In a separate bowl stir together both flours, baking soda, cinnamon, and salt. Add to the wet ingredients and blend well. Stir in 2 cups of mixed dried fruits and pour into prepared baking pan.

4. Bake 50 to 60 minutes, until a toothpick inserted into the center comes out dry, or the top of the bread feels firm when lightly pressed. Keeps several days at room temperature.

INSIDER TIPS
- This recipe is perfect for using up the odds 'n ends in your pantry.
- Sprinkle top with more coconut or streusel (Chapter 15).

CATEGORIES
- Whole grain
- Dairy free
- Nut free

Lemon Tea Cake

This loaf, more like a pound cake, is the only recipe I ever got from a customer. Unfortunately I can no longer remember her name but I do remember requesting the recipe. Really, it's that good.

Yield: 1 9x5-inch loaf pan

- ½ pound (2 sticks) butter
- 1 ¾ cups sugar
- 3 large eggs
- 1 teaspoon lemon extract
- ½ teaspoon vanilla extract
- grated zest of 1 lemon
- ¼ cup lemon juice, preferably fresh-squeezed (about 1 large lemon)
- ¼ cup sour cream
- 2 ½ cups flour
- ¼ teaspoon baking soda
- ½ teaspoon salt

Glaze

- ¼ cup water
- ¼ cup lemon juice, preferably fresh squeezed (about 1 large lemon)
- ¼ cup sugar

1. Preheat oven to 350° F. and grease loaf pan.

2. Cream butter and sugar in a medium bowl then beat in eggs, extracts, zest, and lemon juice. Stir in sour cream.

3. In a separate bowl, combine flour, baking soda, and salt. Add to the wet ingredients and mix well.

4. Pour into prepared pan and bake 75 to 90 minutes, until the top feels firm when gently pressed and a toothpick inserted in the center comes out dry.

5. To make the glaze, boil water, lemon juice, and sugar for 1 minute. Pour over warm loaf. Cool before removing from pan. Keeps five days at room temperature.

INSIDER TIPS

- For seasonal changes, add 2 cups blueberries or raspberries and increase flour by ½ cup.
- Add ½ cup mini-chocolate chips.

CATEGORIES

- Nut free

Pumpkin Apple Bread

This moist spicy loaf features seasonal pumpkin and apples.

Yield: 1 8x4-inch loaf pan

- 1 (15-ounce) can pumpkin puree
- 1 ¼ cups sugar
- ½ cup oil
- 2 large eggs
- ¼ cup water or juice
- 1 ½ cups whole wheat pastry flour
- 1 teaspoon baking soda
- ½ teaspoon salt
- 2 teaspoons cinnamon
- ½ teaspoon nutmeg
- ½ cup raisins
- 1 small apple, finely chopped with skin

1. Preheat oven to 350° F. and grease pan.
2. Mix together pumpkin, sugar, oil, eggs, and water in a medium bowl.
3. In a separate bowl stir together flour, baking soda, salt, cinnamon, and nutmeg. Add to the liquid ingredients. Stir in raisins and apple.
4. Spoon batter into pan and bake 40 to 50 minutes until a deep golden brown and a finger pressed gently on top leaves no imprint. Keeps five days at room temperature.

INSIDER TIPS
- Instead of pumpkin, use 1½ cups of any orange pulp winter squash, such as acorn, butternut, or carnival. To cook squash, cut in half, scoop out seeds and lay face down in glass baking dish. Pour in small amount of orange juice or water to cover bottom of dish. Cook in microwave on high for 12 to 15 minutes or in the oven (350-375° F.) for 45 to 60 minutes. The pulp should be very soft. If it's not done, cook longer. Cool and scrape pulp into a bowl.
- Add 1 tablespoon fresh grated ginger.
- Substitute chopped dates for the raisins.

CATEGORIES
- Dairy free
- Nut free

Sweet Potato Loaf

This quickbread has a beautiful golden color, tender cake-like crumb, and a sweet, luscious flavor. It bakes with an attractive split along the top.

Yield: 1 9x5-inch loaf pan

- 1 cup mashed cooked sweet potatoes, cooled (fresh or canned)
- ½ cup oil
- 1 cup sugar
- 2 large eggs
- ²/₃ cup milk
- 2 teaspoons vanilla
- 2 ½ cups flour
- 1 tablespoon baking powder
- 2 teaspoons cinnamon
- ½ teaspoon salt

1. Preheat oven to 350° F. and grease loaf pan.

2. Beat together potato, oil, sugar, eggs, milk, and vanilla in a medium bowl.

3. In a separate bowl stir together flour, baking powder, cinnamon, and salt, then stir into wet ingredients.

4. Pour into prepared pan and bake 60 to 70 minutes, until the top feels firm when gently pressed and a toothpick inserted near the center comes out clean. Keeps several days at room temperature.

INSIDER TIPS
- Quick fix
- Add ½ cup currants or raisins.
- Top with streusel (Chapter 15) before baking.
- Instead of milk, substitute apple juice.

CATEGORIES
- Nut free

Zucchini Bread

This loaf has a soft, tight, even grain so it can be cut into thin slices.

Yield: 1 9x5-inch loaf pan

- ½ cup oil
- ½ cup applesauce
- 1 ¼ cups sugar
- 2 large eggs
- 2 teaspoons vanilla
- 2 cups whole wheat pastry flour
- 1 ½ cups all-purpose flour
- 1 teaspoon baking soda
- ½ teaspoon baking powder
- ½ teaspoon salt
- 2 teaspoons cinnamon
- ½ teaspoon allspice
- 2-3 cups grated zucchini (1 medium)

1. Preheat oven to 350° F. and grease pan.

2. Beat together oil, applesauce, sugar, eggs, and vanilla in a large bowl.

3. In a separate bowl mix together both flours, baking soda, baking powder, salt, cinnamon, and allspice.

4. Add dry ingredients to the wet and mix thoroughly, then mix in zucchini. Batter will be thick.

5. Pour into prepared pan and bake 60 to 75 minutes, until a toothpick inserted into center comes out dry and the top feels firm when lightly pressed. Keeps one week in fridge.

INSIDER TIPS
- Quick fix
- Add 1 cup chopped dates.
- This recipe makes excellent muffins or cupcakes.

CATEGORIES
- Whole grain
- Dairy free
- Nut free

Chapter 14

Stale Products, Crumbs, and other Leftovers

Once your business is up and running you will likely have excess products that can't be sold. Sometimes you can give these goods away as donations or cut them up for samples, but sometimes you have way too much. And soon enough, the novelty of endless baked goods will wear off on your household residents, extended family, and friends. This is a common problem. Most established bakeries have created recipes to use up this excess. Through their ingenuity and my tested recipes, this chapter provides a bakery recycling program for using your surplus goods.

The first thing to know is to save your unsold, broken, and stale **cookies** in a large sealed tub. Make crumbs by whatever method appeals to you: grind in a food processor, put in a bag and crush with your hands or a rolling pin, or whack 'em with a hammer. Keep highly spiced cookies separate from other flavors.

Cheesecake crust is the simplest way to incorporate excess product. No recipe necessary. Simply press cookie crumbs into the bottom of your prepared pan. Since most cookies are made with fat and sweetener, you don't need to add butter or sugar to the crumbs, the way we do with graham crackers. For large cheesecakes, use an amount equal to the amount of graham cracker crumbs recommended for that size pan. For smaller muffin-size cheesecakes, use a tablespoon measure and drop the crumbs into each paper cup. When all the cups have crumbs, slide the pan back and forth to settle the crumbs evenly in each cup. Use another paper cup and press down on top of each crumb-filled cup.

You can also use cookie crumbs to replace vanilla wafers and graham cracker crumbs in most recipes such as Rum Balls (recipe follows) or the classic bar that goes under several names: Magic Bars, Seven Layer Bars, or Hello Dolly Bars (again, recipe follows). Or sprinkle cookie crumbs over pie or tart crust before adding fruit. It adds a depth of flavor in addition to soaking up excess liquid.

For excess **cakes**, use crumbs as decoration. Scrap off filling and frosting, let cake dry out and crumble into small pieces. Either toast in a low oven or leave open on a cookie sheet. When dry, make into small crumbs. Use these to decorate sides or tops of cakes. I like to use chocolate cake crumbs sprinkled on cupcakes and frosted cakes instead of jimmies. You may also use cake crumbs for sprinkling over pastry dough (pie crust, strudels, Danish, etc.) before adding the fruit filing. As with cookie crumbs, cake crumbs will help soak up excess moisture.

Labeling for these products can be tricky. Many companies, when they use a mixed ingredient product such as these, add every possible ingredient to their label. A label made with crumbs will state "may include the following ingredients" before adding a long list.

Some of the recipes provide no specific amounts because it depends upon the amount of leftovers you have to work with. You decide quantity. My intent with those recipes is to show you how to make a new product from your leftovers.

Amaretto Balls

Amaretto or Rum Balls

Use up lots of cookie crumbs with this bakeshop version of the popular Bourbon or Rum Ball recipes which use store-bought wafer cookies. Wrapping these balls in colored foil is a nice finish and draws attention to their elegance.

Yield: several dozen depending upon your preferred portion size

- ¼ pound (1 stick) butter
- 2 cups confectioners' sugar
- ¼ cup corn syrup
- ¹/₃ cup Amaretto or rum
- 1 ½ teaspoons almond or vanilla extract
- ½ cup cocoa
- 4 cups cookie crumbs
- ½ cup chopped nuts, optional

1. In a large bowl combine butter, sugar, corn syrup, liquor, extract, cocoa, and cookie crumbs. If the mixture is too wet and cannot hold its shape when formed in balls, add more crumbs. If too dry and crumbly, add more corn syrup or liquor (no sampling while you work, or the health inspector will certainly chose this day to show up). Add nuts, if using.

2. Divide dough using a small scoop or 2-tablespoon measure. Place balls close together on a lined tray. This can be a messy job. (Don't lick your fingers!) If it's too sticky, refrigerate first or periodically wet the scoop and/or your hands. The crumbs will eventually soak up some of the moisture. Cover tray and refrigerate for several hours.

3. To finish, roll balls in confectioners' sugar, nuts, or cocoa; or dip each in melted chocolate; or wrap balls completely in colored foil pieces. Wide rolls of food-grade colored foil are available in the baking section of craft supply stores. (You can purchase pre-cut foil pieces but they are way more expensive.)

4. Keeps one week at room temperature, several weeks in fridge.

INSIDER TIPS
- Quick fix
- Substitute any liquor for the rum or Amaretto. Coffee liqueur is another popular seller.
- You may also roll balls in jimmies or coconut.
- Display and serve in small paper candy cups.

Banana Split Trifle

This is another one of those classic recipes that always sold well. I used any light-colored cake, sweetbread, or pound cake. The parfait-style appearance looks impressive in extra tall clear plastic cups, with lids that allow the cherry stem to sit upright.

Yield: 12 individual trifles; use tall decorative plastic ware or cups, with lids

- (2) 8- or 9-inch cakes, or (1) 9x13-inch cake, or (2) pound cakes
- 2-3 medium bananas
- ¼ cup orange juice
- 1 quart strawberries
- 1 (3.5-ounce) package instant chocolate pudding mix
- 2 cups milk
- ¼ cup chopped or sliced nuts
- 12 fresh cherries with stems, or 12 maraschino cherries

1. Cut cake into cubes and divide half of the cake amongst the cups. (You may have extra cake when finished.)

2. Slice bananas and toss with orange juice to coat. Slice berries. Mix pudding and milk. Top cake pieces with half the bananas, half the strawberries, and half the pudding. Repeat, ending with pudding.

3. Sprinkle nuts over top of each cup and add a cherry. Put stem in upright position. Keeps two or three days in fridge.

INSIDER TIPS
- Make substitutions based on available fruit. Blueberries, peaches, and plums also work well.
- Use brownies instead of cake.
- Double pudding amount if desired.

Bread Pudding

Bread pudding is an old stand-by. For an upscale appearance, bake in round cake pans and sell by the wedge. I based my recipe on custard proportions: two eggs for every cup of milk.

Yield: 1 8x8-inch pan

- 2-3 cups stale bread, white or whole wheat
- 4 large eggs
- ½ cup sugar
- 2 cups milk
- 1 teaspoon vanilla
- 1 teaspoon cinnamon
- ½ cup dried fruit, optional

1. Preheat oven to 350° F. and grease pan.

2. Tear bread into small pieces and place in a medium bowl.

3. Beat eggs, sugar, milk, vanilla, and cinnamon in another bowl. Pour over bread and stir.

4. If the bread soaks up all the moisture, add ½ cup more milk. If too wet, add more bread.

5. Bake 40 to 60 minutes, until pudding begins to puff and turns a light golden brown.

6. Can be eaten or sold at any temperature. Store refrigerated, up to three days.

INSIDER TIPS
- Quick fix
- Sell with a hard sauce.
- If you make sweet yeasted pastry, use instead of bread.
- For seasonal changes, add a cup or two of fresh fruit, particularly pears or peaches.
- Add 1 cup (6-ounce bag) chocolate chips.
- Bake in individual disposable pans.

CATEGORIES
- Nut free

Cake Balls or Cookie Balls

When you have a lot of extra cake or cookies, these trendy and popular treats are a perfect way to use them.

Yield: several dozen depending upon your preferred portion size

- (1) 8- or 9-inch cake, crumbled; or 2-3 cups cookie crumbs
- 1 cup frosting or jam
- milk
- melted chocolate for dipping
- sprinkles, optional

1. In a medium bowl, mix crumbs with frosting or jam. Refrigerate for several hours. This will give crumbs a chance to soak up moisture and make it easier to handle.

2. Remove from fridge and test the mixture by scooping a little with a spoon. If it holds together it's fine. If too dry and crumbly add milk, and if too wet, mix in more crumbs.

3. When ready to scoop, line a cookie tray with waxed paper or parchment and place balls close together on the tray. If the crumbs are very sticky and hard to work with, wet your hands in-between making the balls. I set a little bowl of water next to the tray, dip my fingers in, then shake them before handling the mixture. Any extra water shouldn't hurt your final product. Make balls about 1 or 1 ½ inches in diameter. Refrigerate or freeze until ready to dip.

4. Melt chocolate and dip each ball, then place on a lined cookie sheet. Leave a little room in between each one. If using sprinkles, add before the chocolate sets.

5. Keeps several days or weeks. Since ingredients vary, do shelf life testing (Chapter 2).

INSIDER TIPS
- To make cake pops, insert sticks when they're cold, but before they're frozen. Dip entire ball in chocolate. For serving or selling, place top side down in a paper muffin cup.
- Decorate balls with piping or little candies.
- Package in small candy boxes. Don't forget the doilies.

Candy Cups

These look just like peanut butter cups. There are several steps but the results are worthwhile, especially since you'll use up your excess products.

Yield: several dozen cups, varies depending upon how many cake crumbs you have

- chocolate
- cake crumbs
- jam or frosting
- 2 pieces for each cup: chocolate chips, nuts or dried fruit, crystallized ginger or candy
- liquor, optional

1. Use foil or waxed candy cups, which are stronger than paper muffin cups. Place cups on a cookie sheet.

2. Melt chocolate and pour approximately 1 tablespoon into every cup. Pick up each cup and rotate and swirl melted chocolate up the sides. Don't worry about being exact because the top layer of chocolate will cover any imperfections. Let harden at room temperature, or refrigerate 5 minutes for fast set-up.

3. Combine cake with jam or frosting by mashing with a rubber spatula. Add 1 or 2 tablespoons of liquor. The mixture won't need much, so be cautious. Less is more.

4. When chocolate is hard, scoop a small amount of cake mixture into each cup, pressing down to fill entire area. Again, you won't need much.

5. Top each cup with a piece of chocolate, nut, fruit, or candy. Press into cake crumbs and smooth over.

6. When you have filled all cups, pour about 1 tablespoon melted chocolate over the top of each one. Rotate so the chocolate flows to all sides. Top each cup with another piece of fruit, chocolate, candy, or nut to identify the item inside.

7. These keep refrigerated for several weeks depending upon ingredients. Make sure to do shelf life testing (Chapter 2).

INSIDER TIPS

- Promote the cups as a specialty items. You don't have to tell customers these are made of leftover scraps, which diminishes your product.
- This is your chance to create a signature product by combining a unique mixture of texture and flavors.
- Use the Peanut Butter Bars recipe in this chapter to make your own Peanut Butter Candy Cup.
- Any leftover melted chocolate can be used in the next recipe for Chocolate Medallions.

Chocolate Medallions

Whenever we finished dipping our cookies in melted chocolate there were many crumbs mixed in with the remaining chocolate. So we added other ingredients and created a new product.

Mix melted chocolate with nuts, coconut pieces, marshmallows, dried fruits, or pretzels. Drop equal-sized coated pieces onto a sheet of waxed paper or foil. Let these medallions harden at room temperature or refrigerate if necessary. Keeps several months if well-wrapped and placed under lock and key.

INSIDER TIPS
- Quick fix
- Make Sweet 'n Salty Medallions using salted nuts.
- Display and sell in waxed candy cups.

CATEGORIES
- Egg free
- Gluten free

Magic Bars

Also called Seven Layer Bars or Hello Dollys, these are a rich, candy-like bar.

Yield: 1 8x8-inch pan

- ¼ pound (1 stick) butter, melted
- 1 ¾ cups cookie crumbs
- 1 cup (6-ounce bag) chocolate chips
- 1 (14-ounce) can sweetened condensed milk
- 1 cup sweetened coconut

1. Preheat oven to 350° F.

2. Mix melted butter and cookie crumbs in a small bowl. Press into bottom of baking pan.

3. Sprinkle chocolate chips over the crust, then pour condensed milk over the top, spreading evenly. Top with coconut.

4. Bake 25 to 35 minutes, until the top is a medium golden brown and the coconut is toasty. Keeps several days at room temperature.

INSIDER TIPS
- Quick fix
- Use other chip varieties instead of chocolate, particularly butterscotch or white chocolate.
- Add ½ cup chopped dried fruit before adding coconut.

CATEGORIES
- Nut free

Marshmallow Treats

This tasty recipe, suggested by one of my salesclerks, was a surprisingly great seller.

Yield: 1 8x8-inch pan

- ¼ cup (½ stick) butter
- 1 (10.5 ounce) package mini-marshmallows or 7-ounce jar marshmallow crème
- 3 cups any breakfast cereal, crisped rice is traditional
- 2 cups cookie crumbs

1. Grease pan.

2. Melt butter over low heat in a heavy-bottomed saucepan. Don't let it turn brown. Add marshmallows and stir until smooth.

3. Pour in cereal and cookie crumbs and stir well.

4. Press into greased pan. Keeps one week.

INSIDER TIPS
- Quick fix
- Nice when made with gluten-free cereal and crumbs.
- Drizzle with melted dark chocolate.

Peanut Butter Bars

A rich candy bar and a great no-bake recipe rolled into one!

Yield: 1 8x8-inch pan

- 1 cup peanut butter
- ½ pound (2 sticks) butter
- 1 teaspoon vanilla
- 3 ½ cups (1 pound) confectioners' sugar
- 1 ½ cups cookie crumbs

Bar Topping

- 2 cups chocolate buttercream (Chapter 15)

1. Grease pan. If you want to lift out the bars for easy cutting, line pan with waxed paper or foil. Use enough to hang over the edges of the pan.

2. In a large bowl, mix peanut butter, butter, vanilla, sugar, and cookie crumbs. Pat into pan.

3. Spread with topping and refrigerate for at least 1 hour.

4. Cut while cold. Keeps several weeks if refrigerated.

INSIDER TIPS

- To make peanut butter cups, use this recipe as filling in the Candy Cup recipe.
- For Peanut Butter Balls: Refrigerate dough for 2 hours or until firm. Scoop into balls. Place on a sheet tray lined with wax paper and refrigerate for at least 15 minutes. Finish by either rolling in finely chopped peanuts or cookie crumbs, or dip in melted chocolate.

Russian Cake

I learned about Russian Cake (or Russian Slice) from reading the bakery trade magazines. It's simply cake and jam pressed into a cake pan. My unique version has a bottom crust.

Yield: 1 8x8-inch pan

- ¼ pound (1 stick) butter
- ¼ cup granulated sugar
- 1 ¼ cups flour
- ½ cup apricot jam
- 1 12-ounce jar strawberry or raspberry jam
- 4 cups cake scraps, preferably more
- ¼ teaspoon rum extract
- buttercream frosting or glaze (Chapter 15)

1. Preheat oven to 350° F. and grease pan.

2. Cream butter, sugar, and flour in a medium bowl. Press into bottom of pan and bake for 20 to 25 minutes until a medium golden brown.

3. Cool crust, then spread with apricot jam and refrigerate for at least 30 minutes. Doing so should help the jam solidify so it doesn't get blended into the cake mixture.

4. For cake mixture, blend together jam, cake scraps, and rum. The texture should be stick, gooey, and dense. Spread on crust and press down evenly. Frost with buttercream or glaze (Chapter 15). Keeps at least one week in fridge.

INSIDER TIPS
- Sprinkle with colorful jimmies or nuts.

Spice Bars

Spanish Spice Bar, made popular by the A&P supermarket chain, contained leftover cake and Danish pastry crumbs. I added a cream cheese icing and my customers loved this spicy cake with a mellow cream cheese topping.

Yield: 1 8x8-inch pan

- 1 ¾ cups cake crumbs
- ½ cup water
- ¼ cup molasses
- ¼ cup brown sugar
- 3 tablespoons oil
- 2 large eggs
- 1 cup flour
- 1 teaspoon baking soda
- ¼ teaspoon salt
- 2 teaspoons cinnamon
- ¼ teaspoon cloves
- buttercream or cream cheese icing (Chapter 15), optional

1. Preheat oven to 375° F. and grease pan.

2. Using a medium bowl, soak cake crumbs in ½ cup water for a few minutes. Do not drain. Mix in molasses, sugar, oil, and eggs.

3. Stir in flour, baking soda, salt, cinnamon, and cloves. If the batter is dense as cookie dough, add 2-4 tablespoons water. If too wet add more cake crumbs.

4. Pour into the prepared pan and bake for 25 to 35 minutes, until a toothpick inserted near the center comes out clean.

5. Ice, glaze, or dust with confectioners' sugar. Keeps one week.

INSIDER TIPS
- Quick fix
- Add 1 chopped apple or pear.
- Add ½ cup raisins.

CATEGORIES
- Nut free

Chapter 15

Streusels and Icings

My theory (in case you haven't noticed) is it's best to cover baked goods with anything that catches the eye. So before baking, I top with sugar granules, nuts, coconut, or oats. After baking, I use string icing, confectioners' sugar, and glaze for additional eye-appeal. Glaze is a thin confectioners' sugar icing that coats a product. String icing is a little thinner than a glaze and is drizzled across a product, to appear like a string crossing over the top and sides.

Streusel is one of the toppings I most often use to dress up baked goods. If you want to make your baking life easier and faster, work ahead. Whip up a large batch and keep it refrigerated in an air-tight container for two or three months. Then whenever you feel like baking, you won't need to bother with also making up the streusel. I've included several versions of this topping. Just pick a favorite and use it for muffins, loaves, and coffeecakes. You can also use it as a topping for fruit crisps or pies.

Streusels

These keep for a few months if refrigerated in well-sealed containers.

Light Streusel

Yield: Makes about 10 cups

- 3 cups sugar
- 6 cups flour
- 1 pound (4 sticks) butter
- 1 tablespoon vanilla

In a large bowl, mix the sugar and flour. Add butter and begin to cream. Add the vanilla in drips to incorporate throughout the mixture. Cream until the batter *starts* to look as if it will clump together. If you keep mixing, it will become a crust and tedious to work back into a streusel. (In that case, use more flour and hand separate.) Do not pack down when storing.

Dark Streusel

Yield: Makes about 7 cups

- 2 cups whole wheat pastry flour
- 2 cups all-purpose flour
- 2 cups sugar
- 1½ teaspoons salt
- 1½ teaspoons cinnamon, optional
- 1 cup oil
- 6 tablespoons water
- 2 cups chopped walnuts, optional

In a large bowl, mix together all dry ingredients. Pour in oil and water and mix thoroughly. Add nuts, if using. This should clump if squeezed together, but separate back into a streusel texture. Add more flour or water to adjust.

Oat Streusel

Yield: Makes about 6 cups

- 2 cups flour
- 2 cups rolled oats, quick or regular
- 1 ½ cups sugar
- ½ teaspoon salt
- ¾ pound (3 sticks) butter, melted

In a large bowl, mix the flour, oats, sugar, and salt. Add the melted butter and mix thoroughly. If too wet, gradually add more flour and/or oats until crumbly.

Buttercream Frostings

Refrigerate leftovers for up to three weeks.

Vanilla Buttercream

Yield: Makes about 3 cups

- ¼ pound (1 stick) butter
- ½ cup vegetable shortening
- 3 ½ cups (1 pound) confectioners' sugar
- 1 tablespoon vanilla
- 2-3 tablespoons milk

Beat butter and shortening, then beat in sugar. Add vanilla and milk, and beat until the consistency is ready for spreading. Add more milk if too thick.

Cream Cheese frosting – substitute 1 (8-ounce) package cream cheese for the shortening in recipe above.

INSIDER TIPS

For variations to basic vanilla buttercream, spoon as much as needed into a separate bowl and add small amounts of the following. Adjust to taste:

- Spice frosting – stir in cinnamon
- Coffee frosting – stir in instant coffee powder
- Raspberry frosting – stir in raspberry jam
- Maple frosting – stir in maple extract

Chocolate Buttercream

Yield: Makes about 3 cups

- ¼ pound (1 stick) butter
- ½ cup vegetable shortening
- 6 tablespoons cocoa
- 3 ½ cups (1 pound) confectioners' sugar
- 1 tablespoon vanilla
- 4-6 tablespoons milk

Beat butter and shortening, then beat in cocoa and sugar. Add vanilla and milk, and beat until the consistency is ready for spreading. Add more milk if too thick.

Glazes and String Icings

These harden to the touch so any wrapping will not stick, as it does with buttercream frosting.

Vanilla Glaze

Yield: Makes about 1 cup, enough for 2 coffeecakes or 12 cupcakes

- 1 ½ cups confectioners' sugar
- 2 tablespoons butter, melted
- 2-3 tablespoons water or milk
- 1 teaspoon vanilla

In medium bowl, combine all ingredients and mix until smooth.
For variations to basic vanilla glaze, stir in small amounts of the following, then adjust to taste:

- Spice glaze – stir in cinnamon
- Coffee glaze – stir in instant coffee powder
- Fruit glaze – use fruit juice or (warmed) jelly instead of water
- Maple frosting – stir in maple extract

For **Vanilla String Icing**, thin glaze with water.

Chocolate Glaze

Yield: Makes about 1 cup, enough for 2 coffeecakes or 12 cupcakes

- 1 cup confectioners' sugar
- $^1/_3$ cup cocoa
- 2 tablespoons butter, melted
- 2-3 tablespoons milk
- 1 teaspoon vanilla extract

In medium bowl, combine all ingredients and mix until smooth.
For **Chocolate String Icing**, thin glaze with water.

Semi-Sweet Chocolate Glaze

Yield: Makes about 1 cup, enough for 2 coffeecakes or 12 cupcakes
- ½ cup chocolate chips
- ½ cup chocolate wafers
- 2 tablespoons butter

Melt all ingredients together and pour over top of cake, letting it roll down cake sides.

APPENDICES

Pan Capacity

Pan capacity refers to volume – how much liquid a pan holds when filled to the top. Since manufacturers' sizes are not standardized the following chart is meant only as a guide. To measure your pan capacity, fill with water to top. For baking, fill with batter only ½ to ²/₃ full. Don't overfill a pan or the batter will overflow sides and/or sink in the middle. When in doubt, add less batter.

2 cups	5x3-inch small loaf pan
3 cups	5-inch bundt pan
	7 x 3-inch loaf pan
	6-inch bundt pan
4 cups	8-inch round cake pan
	8 x 4-inch loaf pan
	9-inch round cake pan
	9-inch pie plate
6 cups	8 x 2-inch round cake pan
	8.5 x 4.5-inch loaf pan
	11 x 7-inch baking dish
	8-inch square baking dish
	9 x 1.5-inch round cake pan
8 cups	11 x 7-inch baking dish
	9-inch square baking dish
	9 x 2-inch round cake pan
	9 x 2-inch deep dish pie plate
	10-inch pie plate
	9 x 5-inch loaf pan
10 cups	9-inch tube pan
	10-inch bundt pan
	10-inch round cake pan
	10 x 15 x 1-inch jellyroll pan
12 cups	9 x 13-inch baking dish
	10-inch tube pan
	10 x 3.5-inch bundt pan
	10-inch springform pan
15 cups	9 x 13 x 2-inch baking dish

Disher/Scoop Capacity

For Portion Control

In commercial food production, *dishers,* commonly called *scoops* or *ice cream scoops,* are used to create consistent product sizes. As a result, portion size is controlled so that every portion has the same ingredient cost.

Most manufacturers use a common color-coding and numbering system, although there is a slight capacity variation amongst brands.

Below are the nine most popular sizes. If you need something smaller than the orchid 40, the scooping process becomes tedious. Try using a larger scoop and then divide each one by hand. For instance, if you need a 1 tablespoon amount, scoop all of your dough with yellow 20, then use your fingers to divide each ball of dough into thirds. I do this for small cookies and candies and have found it to be much faster than using a 1 tablespoon scoop.

Size	Color	Fluid ounces	Practical usage batter or dough, rounded to nearest practical measure
6	White	5.33	²/₃ cup
8	Gray	4.0	½ cup
10	Ivory	3.2	6 tablespoons
12	Green	2.66	¹/₃ cup
16	Blue	2.0	¼ cup
20	Yellow	1.6	3 tablespoons
24	Red	1.333	2 ½ tablespoons
30	Black	1.067	2 tablespoons
40	Orchid	0.8	1 ½ tablespoons

Fluid ounces
0.5 = 1 tablespoon
1.0 = 2 tablespoons

To use: Dip scoop into the dough, filling to capacity. Drag over the edge of the bowl or use your other hand to scrape the surface, then use the thumb release to drop dough onto your baking sheet.

11604521R0012

Made in the USA
Lexington, KY
18 October 2011